T0386065

LIVERPOOL:
A MEMOIR OF WORDS

LIVERPOOL:
A MEMOIR OF WORDS

TONY CROWLEY

LIVERPOOL UNIVERSITY PRESS

First published 2023 by
Liverpool University Press
4 Cambridge Street
Liverpool
L69 7ZU

British Library Cataloguing-in-Publication data
A British Library CIP record is available

ISBN 978-1-83764-438-4

Typeset by Carnegie Book Production, Lancaster
Printed and bound by CPI Group (UK) Ltd, Croydon CR0 4YY

For
Tom Mulhearn
and
Mark Ord
good friends both

CONTENTS

ACKNOWLEDGMENTS

Given the nature of this project, in order to acknowledge my debts properly I would have to thank an inordinate number of people, many of whom are unknown to me; I therefore express general gratitude to all of them. I can, however, name specific people to whom I am indebted for help and support with this work, but also in various other ways. They include: Fazia Aitel, Jasmine Andersson, John Belchem, Bridget Bennett, Nigel Boyle and Vanessa Ashworth, Deborah Cameron, Joe Cleary, John Corness, Karen Corrigan, Frank Cottrell-Boyce, David Crystal, Tony Evans, Catherine Green, Emma Harding, Gail Hershatter, Patrick Honeybone, Hao and Rachel Huang, Brian Kenny, John Kerrigan, Grace Laurencin, Andrew Lees, Andrew Long, Jen McCarthy, Ron and Janet McCauley, Ann McKee, Peter McKee, Andrew McNeillie, Louise McWatt, the Midghalls one and all – Gary, Marion, Mark, Paula, Shirley and Yvonne – Deborah Mulhearn, Rachel Mulhearn, Susan Mulhearn, Tom Mulhearn, Janet Muller, Nicholas Murray, Tim Murray, Bernard and Heather O'Donoghue, Francis O'Gorman, Michael O'Neill (RIP), Billy and Lily Ord (RIP), Tom Paulin, John Peacock, Angela Poingdestre, Elsa and Bruce Robbins, Peter Robinson, Gill Rowlands, Ray Ryan, Dion and Megan Scott-Kakures, Stephen Sheedy, Paddy Shennan, Julia Snell, Kate Spowage, Jane Taylor, Liam Thorpe, Peter Trudgill, Sheila Walker, Bernard and Mary Weston, and John Whale. I am also grateful to Anthony Cond and the staff at Liverpool University Press, to my editor Christabel Scaife, and to my colleagues in the School of

English at the University of Leeds. Special thanks are due to Sheila Turner and the Williamson Art Gallery and Museum for permission to use *Cathedral from Weller Street, Toxteth, Liverpool* for the cover.

The dead are a presence in this text, and I know that Con Crowley and Marie Midghall are never far from the thoughts of those who loved them and those they loved. I am as ever grateful to my siblings – Nicky, Colette, Terry and Jacky – to my nephews and nieces – Jack, Ellie, Tom, Mattie, Helen, Rory, Erin and Roisín – and to Teddy and Ann Crowley. Geneviève and Michael Cuming have always given me their unstinting love and encouragement, and I thank them for it. But the most profound debt is to Emily, for her love, faith and support, and to our children, Joseph and Louise, for the wonder they inspire, the laughter they bring, and the love they engender. I also have to thank the kids for their introduction to some of the new words and meanings that their generation has produced though, as I am sure they would say, that's 'calm' but not 'deep' (I can see them rolling their eyes already).

INTRODUCTION:
OUR COMMON LANGUAGE

'The place a memory, the memory a place'

Matt Simpson, 'Blossom Street', *An Elegy for the*
Galosherman (1990: 75)

Liverpool English: a glocal language

It's hard to come from Liverpool and not feel that you have
a distinctive way of speaking. But of course that perception
only comes gradually; growing up, the language we spoke was
just ... well, the language we spoke. And, like everyone else, I
was born into the language of others. I did not start speaking
on my own, nor was there a magical leap into developed
consciousness. As with each of us, the development of my
language from infancy (*in fans* – without speech) was gradual
and consisted in the slow labour of articulation – the joining
together of meaningful sounds – principally by means of the
deceptively complex process of imitation. So many voices
helped to form my voice: my very individuality was derived
from my socialization into the language practices of the
community in which I was raised. And so, although I call it
'my language', the language was there before me, and it will
outlast me: it is mine and alien to me at one and the same
time.

Of course the signs into which I first grew were those of my immediate family and neighbours and, as far as I remember, it was rare to hear other forms, except of course on the radio or television (though, truth be told, in the early 1960s there didn't appear to be much of either). Things changed once school began – St Malachy's in the Dingle and then St Francis of Assisi in Garston – and soon the first articulations were heard of different forms of speech, accents of authority, voices to be listened to; it was the beginning of the disciplining of our tongues. I imagine that most of our primary school teachers spoke with some form of local speech, though some we heard distinctly as 'not from round here' or, more damningly, 'from London' (a general and probably inaccurate attribution meaning somewhere 'from the South' – though that too was an inaccurate, homogenizing phrase). It was certainly the case that even the local teachers sounded different enough from us for it to be clear that their status was elevated. The headmistress at St Francis, for example, sounded what we called 'Allerton posh', a perception I was amused to verify many years later on meeting her by chance. She congratulated me for 'getting on' – her phrase – by going to university. 'Getting on' is a curiously non-specific phrase, of course, and I've never been quite sure what it means. But then people do say those sorts of things: when I was a lecturer I was once told by a senior colleague that I had 'escaped my Liverpudlian working-class upbringing'. I was irked and puzzled by the verb; my particular childhood and education had nurtured and formed me – there was nothing to 'escape' from. Anyway my headmistress had obviously forgotten (I hadn't) her prediction, delivered to my parents in her office when I was nine, that I would fail the eleven-plus exam. Still, 'Allerton posh' is what she was – I remember her fluting voice leading the singing of the anthem we sang just before the summer holidays. It began with 'Mother of all that is pure and glad, all that is bright and blest', and ended with the words 'Causa nostrae laetitiae' ('Source of our joy'). To a child we sang 'cows nostrils'. We were indeed small, with no Latin and less Greek.

Growing up in the early 1960s in a working-class area in the South End of Liverpool (the place and time matter), the language I acquired was made up of the words and sounds of a very particular location at a given time. It was a local language – but then all languages are located – and yet also a national language, and, though I didn't know it, a so-called 'global language'. I am suspicious of that curious label for a number of reasons, but principally because such glib phrases are always deeply ideological. Indeed, one thing that a lifetime researching language has taught me is that the ways we reflect on, speak about, and write about language are political, in the sense that they carry with them social attitudes, values, predispositions. This ideological baggage is often obscured, because the terms and concepts that we use to describe language appear natural and thus neutral; but they are not. 'Global English' is a good example of this process. Though it is a familiar term these days, it was coined in the 1940s at a time of changing relations between 'British English' and 'American English' (and, of course, Britain and America). It was first used to refer to a form of English written in a new 'global alphabet'. It was only in the 1990s that 'Global English' started to signify 'a form of English used internationally' – a meaning that was created by an unholy alliance of 'English as a foreign language' teaching organizations (which made what was once the preserve of the British Council and amateur language schools into a vast profit-driven industry), professionals in linguistics (never slow to spot a line to keep the business going), and the British state (in the form of the 'soft power' exercised by the Ministry of Trade).

If 'Global English' bears the traces of a particular phase in history, and a specific politics of language, the same can be said of other terms used to describe the dominant language spoken and written in the British Isles. 'British English', for example, far from being a recent coinage (as most linguists appear to suppose), was a mid nineteenth-century neologism, first used to draw a distinction with 'American English'. 'American English', in turn, was coined by Noah Webster, the linguist of American Independence, in the preface to his *Compendious Dictionary of the English Language* (1806): 'in fifty years from this time, the American-English will be spoken by more people, than all the other dialects of the language' (the dropping of the hyphen over time tells us a lot about the status of the form). Webster's project was conceptually pre-empted by the coinage of 'Americanism' in 1781 by John Witherspoon (a Scot who became President of Princeton): 'Americanisms, by which I understand a use of phrases or terms, or a construction of sentences, even among persons of rank and education, different from the use of the same terms or phrases, or the construction of similar sentences, in Great Britain'. Witherspoon's position was complicated: he defended linguistic variation and held that America would develop a 'centre or standard of our own'. But given that this had not yet occurred (Webster's work was to become the authority), Witherspoon listed what he called American 'improprieties'. 'Americanism', he explained, 'which I have coined for the purpose, is exactly similar in its formation and signification to the word Scotticism' (Witherspoon 1781: 1). 'Scotticism', used by Daniel Defoe in the early eighteenth century, simply meant a word that didn't count as what might be called 'English English' and was therefore stigmatized. 'English English' also bore the marks of colonial struggle (as does its counterpart, 'Irish English'). Both first appear in the Irish dramatist Charles Macklin's *The True-Born Irishman* (1783): 'Let me have our own good plain, old Irish English, which I insist upon is better than all the English English that ever coquets and coxcombs brought into the land' (Macklin 1783: 46).

The point of these examples is to show that the terms and categories that we use to describe forms of language (such as 'Global English', 'British English', 'American English', 'Americanism', 'Irish English', 'English English' and, yes, 'Liverpool English' and 'Scouse'), are not ahistorical, but produced for specific historical purposes and, for that very reason, they have to be treated with caution, not to say suspicion. For example, I have concerns about the glib use of the phrase 'Global English', because of the unexamined politics that lie behind it. The fact is, English may be used internationally, but it isn't (it really isn't) 'global' – and so the danger is that 'Global English' can be used as an unwitting instrument for yet another covert neo-imperial fantasy. I also have another objection to 'Global English', which is its vagueness (which form of English is 'Global English?'). For, as a matter of historical reality, the speech I grew up in and with, the language of Liverpool (popularly known as 'Scouse'), was itself 'global' in a specific sense of the term. Because, over a long period, that language had been forged by people from all over the world who were in various forms of contact (including emigration, trade, cultural communication) with and within a town that grew from a small fishing port in the early eighteenth century to become 'the gateway of Empire' not two centuries later. Truth be told, the vernacular language in which I was brought up was a product of a mode of cultural openness to the world predicated on a very specific, sometimes glorious, sometimes bitterly tragic, history with world-wide implications and consequences. Scratch the local in this case, as in so many others, and you find the global.

If Liverpool was 'the gateway to Empire', then its history illustrates the simple but often overlooked point that its gates didn't just open outwards (it was also 'the gateway from Empire'). In fact the port was the conduit for a 'continual influx of strangers', as William Enfield, one of Liverpool's first historians, put it in *An Essay Towards the History of Leverpool* (1773). Those strangers came to the city by work, trade and military routes that crossed land, sea and ocean. They came from near: from Lancashire, Cheshire, and other areas of England, Wales, Ireland and Scotland. They came from further away: from Italy, Germany, Russia, Scandinavia. And they came from further still: from the Arab world, Africa, India, China, the United States of America ... And all of them brought their languages with them – their words, and their specific sounds. They also brought their cultures – or at least aspects of their cultures. I grew up with some of these 'strangers', who were also neighbours, acquaintances, friends, shopkeepers, people you met in the street. Ali, from Morocco, who ran the tiny corner shop in Prophet Street (where I was born, on an armchair, while my dad rang for the midwife from the phone-box on Northumberland Street). The Italian-American family who lived in the tenements on Essex Street, opposite Prophet Street. Lascar (Indian) seamen who lodged in a hostel round the corner, on Mill Street. And the strange crowd who gathered just across Park Road every Sunday in their 'bezzies' (best clothes), speaking a language that none of us understood or even recognized (in the enormous, forbidding, Welsh Congregational church, Sunday services were said in Welsh, which was the second language of Liverpool at the end of the nineteenth century). Later, at St Francis's, many of the kids were Irish – and Liverpool Irish, which is a different group altogether – often from large families (testimony to the fearful grip of Catholic teaching on our parents). And at St Edward's College, the state-funded Catholic grammar school that I attended, there was one black pupil who carried a name as indisputably Irish as 'Paddy Murphy'. The story was that his father was a (Kru) sailor who had abandoned his Liverpool Irish mother (hence the name). Italian-Americans, Lascars, Welsh, Kru, Irish ... elements in a mode of everyday complexity, which we called, for short, 'Liverpudlian'.

On the other hand, that homogenizing term, 'Liverpudlian', should not mask particular forms of difference. Multiculturalism was a historical fact (rather than a political goal) and it was hardly an easy-going, liberal, nicey-nicey way of life. It was a complicated, multivalent, sometimes joyful, sometimes antagonistic, sometimes divisive, sometimes communal, mode of lived experience. In fact, the Liverpool in which I grew up was stratified spatially by class and ethnicity and the cultural distinctions they engender. In that respect it was like many British cities, but it also had the added element of sectarianism, which is typical of only a few. Given Liverpool's appalling history of racism and sectarianism, it was inevitable that part of growing up in the city entailed the acquisition of a knowledge of the spatial contours of racial and sectarian power relations: which areas, or streets within areas, belonged to which group, the bounties and dangers of crossing boundaries, the benefits and costs of trespass. The city was marked by elaborate patterns of identity and allegiance that were the legacy of deep historical forces (colonialism in Ireland, the Empire and slavery, class formation), but which were played out at the level of everyday practice. The stratification of Liverpool is complex and spatial delineation is intricate and convoluted at times. What strikes me now is how small the space was in which the effects and after-effects of history forged us: a few hundred yards could demarcate areas whose boundaries were clear and recognized. At a larger scale, evidently, the South End isn't the North End, although both terms originally referred to no more than areas of the city centre; but even within these general designations there are great disparities. For example, though both are in the South End, the Dingle isn't Allerton (and Allerton and Garston, though contiguous, are socially distinct). What's more, no one from Liverpool would be ignorant of the social connotations attached to each of these place-names (socio-onomastics, to give it the technical term). Indeed, part of being 'from' Liverpool is knowing this pattern of significance.

There are linguistic differences too between districts of the city, as the editors of the first glossary of Liverpool English, *Lern Yerself Scouse: How to Talk Proper in Liverpool* (Shaw 1966), found to their cost. This folk-linguistic (and historically important) introduction to Liverpool speech was based, apparently inadvertently, on 'Dingle Scouse, from the south-end'. Such was the outcry about this wanton misrepresentation of the language of Liverpool that the publisher, the Scouse Press, moved immediately to publish *Lern Yerself Scouse, Vol. 2: The ABZ of Scouse* (1966), which covered 'north-end dialect, or Bootle Scouse' (Spiegl 2000: n.p.). The perception of this variation persists, as in the Liverpool writer Kevin Sampson's *Outlaws* (2001), in which Ged, a Dingleite, and thus a South-Ender, reflects on linguistic difference within the city:

> People in the North End try to say the Dingle lads have our own way of talking, but that's shite, really. We do have sayings and that, to be fair – the lads at the match used to slaughter us for the way we'd say 'a accident' or 'a escort' and that. What we'd do to properly wind them up is we'd drop an aitch an all, too. A amburger and that. A atchet. But we don't talk no different to any other cunt, in fairness. That's the Tocky lads. It's the Granby firm's got the patter, all the black boys and that, all the lads with race, if you will. Now them lads have got their own thing going on. The black lads that we grew up with round the South End, once they got to

a certain age they did all start talking that bit more Yardie, to be fair. They'd be saying 'I axed him' and that instead of 'I asked him'. Perfectly A-OK saying 'I asked him' the year before, but once they started getting older it was all the other thing. 'Ah axthed 'im for thum thkunk.' Putting on a lisp, by the way. Oh yis. *Pretending* to have a speech defect. That was just a handful of them, to be fair – Granby Street and round there. Lisps and Jamaican accents. (Sampson 2001: 24–5)

The discussion here concerns ethnicity and its linguistic effects, though Ged also remarks on the impact of class (or, at least, perceptions of class): 'the Holylands', a network of streets that included Moses Street, Jacob Street, Isaac Street, and David Street, 'was considered posh compared to the other side of Harlow Street'. The physical distances here are small: Dingle Lane is little more than a mile from Granby, and the Holyland is about 500 yards from Harlow Street (beyond which lay Prophet Street). But the perceived social differences are real enough, as are those between the South End and North End, as Ged acknowledges, albeit in a rather self-contradictory manner:

We [Dingleites] haven't really got an accent. We use a bit of backslang, to be fair, now and then and that, but we don't really talk different to the Scotty Road crew. 'Stotty Road', that's what they used to say up there. And 'the Stratford End'. Them North End beauts, always going on about taking the Stratford End, they were. You'd give up telling the cunts it weren't called that. (Sampson 2002: 25)

What Ged is describing here is the social significance, within Liverpool, of pronunciation, style and lexical choice. Words, and the way you say them, matter here just as much as anywhere else.

A hierarchy of language

The roots of the term 'accent' lie with singing (the root is the Latin *cantāre*, 'to sing' – connected to the Greek προσῳδία, *prosodía*, 'a song sung to music'), and it came to mean the marks added to writing to guide pronunciation. The extension of the term to the sense recorded in the *OED* as 'a mode of pronunciation distinctive to a country, area, social class, or individual' is an early modern development. An illustrative (and very early example) is found in *As You Like It* (1599), in which Orlando, denied the courtly upbringing and education that was his by right as a gentleman, and banished to the Forest of Arden, meets Rosalind, daughter of the usurped Duke and similarly exiled to Arden (Rosalind and Orlando had earlier fallen in love, but here Rosalind is in disguise as Ganymede). During the encounter, Orlando asks Rosalind/Ganymede, 'Are you native of this place?'. His curiosity is piqued for a specific reason, as he reveals: 'Your accent is something finer than you could purchase in so removed a dwelling'. To which she replies: 'an old/religious uncle of mine taught me to speak, who was/in his youth an inland man' (Shakespeare 1974: III ii 338–45). The point here is not simply that Ganymede/Rosalind's language reveals social status (which in this case does not quite fit her adopted identity), but that it is evaluated as 'finer' than it should be, thus indicating a discursive order in which some accents are evaluated more favourably than other.

What Shakespeare is depicting is a consequence of the construction of a hierarchy of speech whose origins lie in the late sixteenth century, but which continues to exercise a deep and pernicious influence in British cultural life. One of the first, and most influential, formulations of 'the best English', was George Puttenham's prescription of the model form of speech in his *Arte of English Poesie* (1589). It should be, he asserts, the language which is spoken in the king's Court, or in the good towns and cities within this land, rather than the language of the border areas, or port towns (where strangers gather for the sake of commerce), or even universities, where scholars use too many pretentious words taken from ancient languages, and definitely not the language of country villages or corners of the realm, where you find only poor, rustic, uncivilised people. Also, the writer shouldn't imitate the speech of craftsmen or carters, or anyone else of the inferior class, even if they were raised in, or live in, the best towns or cities of the realm, because they abuse good speech with their accents, mangled pronunciation and false spelling. Poets therefore need to follow the well-bred, the sort that the Greeks call 'charientes' – the civilised and graciously behaved ... They should not use the everyday words used by people from the north, whether they be noblemen, gentlemen, or their best clerks, nor any form of speech used beyond the river Trent, because even though no one can deny that they speak the purest form of Saxon English, their language, like that spoken in the far west of the country, is not so courtly nor modern as our southern English. So, writers should take as their model the usual speech of the court, and that of London and the shires surrounding it, up to a limit of about 60 miles. (My modernized version)

Puttenham's demarcations (not this, not this, not this ... including not 'the language of port towns' – which explains Rosalind's claim that she was taught by 'an inland man') culminate in that stark privileging of 'the usual speech of the Court', London, and the shires within sixty miles (an area that includes Oxford and Cambridge) as the 'best' form of the spoken language. And more or less the same framework was set out in Thomas Sheridan's *A Course of Lectures on Elocution* (1762), another important text in the history of English prescriptivism. For Sheridan the paradigm was to be the speech of 'men of education at court', on the basis that 'all other dialects, are sure marks, either of a provincial, rustic, pedantic or mechanic education; and therefore have some degree of disgrace annexed to them' (Sheridan 1762: 30). The basic assumption in such formulations, consolidated and disseminated through the education system, literature, and various forms of popular culture in the nineteenth and twentieth centuries, is that the spoken norm in Britain is defined in terms of the regional and class identity of a particular group of speakers. It is peculiar, though, to note that, in this form of prescriptivism, the 'best English' is defined negatively (not this, not them), rather than with regard to the specific features of this form that make it 'the best'. In other words, there is no attempt to say why this form of language is the best – no discussion of particular features and their advantages. It is simply 'the best English' because it is spoken by specific people and not others. And yet despite the vacuous circularity of these definitions ('what is the best English? – the English spoken by the best speakers'; 'who are the best speakers? – those who speak the best English') the efficacy and power of this discursive construction is such that, despite its social and geographic basis, an unmarked norm has been established, to which all other forms of speech are compared, and according to which all are evaluated.

It is important to know the history of this hierarchical ordering of language precisely because its effects persist – I come across it on a regular basis in my professional life. Now, it might be imagined that only a remarkable level of ignorance about yourself and the society in which you were raised could persuade anyone living in contemporary Britain to proclaim that they 'don't have an accent'. And yet, though remarkable, such ignorance is hardly uncommon. Teaching a variety of courses on 'language in society' for almost forty years, I've frequently been met with a look that ranges from confused to indignant ('but I don't have an accent'), when I've informed a particular type of student that they do indeed have an accent, like the rest of us. It's a physical embodiment of a form of linguistic privilege, the marker of a type of social status that allows the bearer to view their own speech as the norm and the language of others as an example of 'variation' (as sociolinguists call it). Of course there is a way of thinking about this that views such speakers as victims of the history of British prescriptivism too. And, in a sense, it is true – their self-blindness is the product of a particular tradition that is embedded in everyday life. Why would they know that the sounds that come out of their mouths carry the marks of history just as much as the sounds that come out of anyone else's, given they are told (implicitly but constantly) that their speech is the unmarked/ahistorical/natural/given norm? The difference being, of course, that those who speak one of the marked and stigmatized forms of English are not afforded the privilege of such ignorance. They (we) are all too aware that their language is always-already accented, always-already classed as inferior, always-already non (sub)-standard.

Accents: exceedingly rare and otherwise

Needless to say, of course, nobody, but nobody, from Liverpool could ever be under any illusion that their speech is accented – it's even celebrated in the folk-song, 'In My Liverpool Home':

> In my Liverpool Home,
> We speak with an accent exceedingly rare,
> Meet under a statue exceedingly bare,
> And if you want a Cathedral, we've got one to spare
> In my Liverpool Home.

I don't know when it became clear to me that my accent was un-usual (to use Puttenham's term), though, as noted earlier, I remember being aware in primary school that the voices of some figures of authority – teachers and priests mainly – were different from those I heard at home and in the local neighbourhood. But in many ways my geographic and social world was so limited (in a precise and neutral sense of that term) that my access to linguistic difference was relatively restricted. It was education – at all levels – that was to be the main means by which I gained knowledge of the ways in which my language was evaluated. I may be wrong, but I don't recall negative attitudes towards our speech in my first schools, St Malachy's or St Franny's, both in working-class areas of Liverpool. That all changed at St Edward's College, which drew pupils from all over Liverpool, and indeed St Helens and Widnes, on the basis of the eleven-plus exam (I was actually ten when I started at Sneddies, which made the school motto – 'Viriliter Age', 'act like a man' – a little daunting). At St Edward's I discovered that there were different types of accent within Liverpool that related to both class and the spatial layout of the city (a Southender myself, I came across people who thought of themselves as Northenders for the first time). But I also found out that boys who lived twenty minutes away from the school (places such as Prescot, Rainhill, Cronton, St Helens and Widnes were all on the other side of the dividing line) sounded utterly different and used words I'd never heard. Though I didn't know it, this difference was a result of Liverpool's unique place in what linguists call the British 'dialect continuum', which is the term for the series of contiguous dialects that stretches across England. Within the continuum, neighbouring dialects and accents usually share features as well as having their own distinctive forms, and thus the further apart on the continuum, the greater the differences between the dialects and accents. The exception is Liverpool, which is markedly different from its nearest neighbours and thus something of an anomaly: 'exceedingly rare' indeed.

Sneddies was run by the Christian Brothers and it was there that I first came across that strange practice, which

I've experienced often since, of people feeling that they have the right to mimic your accent when they hear you speak. One Brother in particular would spend lessons repeating everything we said with a sneering mock-Liverpool voice, before pronouncing our words back to us in what he took to be the 'correct' form. It was a curious thing to do, not least because he, along with most people who perform such imitative rudeness, was unable to offer more than a parodic mish-mash of pronunciations, only some of which resembled those that belong to the Liverpool accent. But, if they couldn't sound like us, at least some of the Brothers were apparently determined that we would speak 'proper' like them (which was odd in itself, given that a fair few of the brothers were Irish and spoke accordingly). And so, for the first year of my secondary schooling, I and the other hundred or so Eddies boys in my form were subjected to the strictures of 'speech training' (there's that disciplining of the tongue) by poor Miss Sarath, whose riotous lessons were punctuated by cries of 'what's up with the brown cow?' (our version of 'How now brown cow', a revealingly nonsensical phrase). We could have been in the yard playing footy. No doubt the same impulse that informed the introduction of 'speech training' also lay behind the decision to make us wear bright purple blazers and multicoloured striped ties, and to have rugby union as the school's main sport. That was a telling choice: as predominantly working-class boys, most of us were devoted to footy (though the Widnes and St Helens boys preferred rugby league), so playing rugby union was a coded message about class and culture. All of that said, however, there were teachers at the Eddies who introduced me to the complex riches of the English language and its literature, and others who inculcated in me a love for French and Spanish (which were the subjects I read at university before switching to English). And, for that, I am eternally and profoundly grateful – it is a debt I can never hope to repay. For the lessons in the devaluation of my speech, and that of the people who loved and cared for me, my family, friends and neighbours? Well, I later found that it was part of the very long tradition discussed in the previous section (which remains powerful, even if its upholders have no idea about the history that lies behind it). And besides, it's always good to get an early sense of what you're up against.

I travelled up and down England watching Liverpool football team as a teenager, but I'd crossed few borders before going to Oxford University at the age of seventeen (we went to Wales once for a week for a summer holiday – it rained). Oxford was only three hours away on the train, but to get there you had to cross the most difficult borders of all – the cultural and psychological boundaries that demarcated two distinct worlds. In actuality, Oxford wasn't a different world from working-class Liverpool; it was a different planet inhabited by aliens who spoke a distinct language. There were lots of ways in which social distinction was made clear at Oxford: dress, everyday habits, food, sport, cultural capital and, of course, money .... But one important medium was language. In one sense, of course, there was a positive aspect to this; the very point of going to university is to learn new things, including new terms and concepts – and, again, I am deeply grateful for the help that I was given in broadening my linguistic, intellectual and cultural knowledge. I think on it often. Yet repeatedly during my time there language was the means by which I was made to feel that this wasn't really my world. Occasionally, this was a case of vocabulary – some of my words were met with that polite (or not) stare that suggests that you have committed some sort of linguistic offence. Sometimes it was tone, when I used what I considered to be no more than emphasis, but which was taken as rudeness, or when I heard excessive politeness, which was in fact rudeness (I've since learned to pay attention when listening to the deliberately modulated blandness of the powerful). But, more often than not, it was just the sounds that came from my mouth – my accent – which was on occasion met with surprise, sometimes with simple disdain. One term I came to an agreement with my tutor at another college that we wouldn't meet after week three (there were eight weeks in the term). He said he was unexpectedly busy, but he'd give me the reading, look at my work and then give me a good report (the last bit surprised me, but who was I ...?). The arrangement suited me, so that's what we did. I did the reading and the essays (which he didn't read, as far as I could tell), he got paid, and I received a good report – a very good report in fact. A few years later, one of his colleagues informed me that he hadn't been able to teach me because he 'couldn't stand' my voice during tutorials. What he didn't know, of course, was that the feeling was entirely mutual (I mean, it's hardly as though linguistic prejudice just runs one way now, does it?). For as George Bernard Shaw notes in the preface to *Pygmalion* (1916), a text that takes language politics as its theme, 'it is impossible for an Englishman to open his mouth without making some other Englishman hate or despise him' (Shaw 1916: 3). There is a long history behind that observation, as I alluded to earlier, but the effect of the linguistic and social pressure was real enough in Oxford in the late 1970s. One of my peers from Sneddies also went to Oxford and, by the end of the first term, 'Jimmy' had become 'James' and he'd managed to acquire a version of 'posh' apparently designed to mask his Liverpool origins. It sounded awful; if they couldn't do us, we definitely couldn't do them.

Language attitudes

Linguists have been tracking 'language attitudes' since the 1970s (recent 'national reports' about accent discrimination are a bit late to the party). From then till now, responses towards the Liverpool accent have been consistently negative: it hovers near the bottom, just above the accent associated with Birmingham. It has to be said, however, that there are different ways of reading the responses to the questionnaires used to record the attitudes, since some of them reveal as much about the people who set them as they do about the responses of those surveyed. In 2013, for example, the *Daily Mail* featured an article that reported on a language survey conducted by ITN whose aim was 'to rate accents in terms of friendliness, intelligence and trustworthiness'. The newspaper headline was – 'Scousers have the "least intelligent and least trustworthy" accent' – and the article glossed the survey's findings by noting that 'Liverpudlians sound the least intelligent, according to the research, with an average of 13 per cent voting them 'not at all intelligent', and that 'the Liverpudlian accent was the least trusted, with more people saying that they do not trust it (29 per cent), than do (24 per cent)'. (Woollaston 2013). But it is worth reflecting on the questions that were asked: 'Do you find the Liverpool accent Very friendly/Fairly friendly/Neither friendly nor unfriendly/Not very friendly/Not at all friendly/Don't know?' and 'Do you find the Liverpool accent Very intelligent/Fairly intelligent/Neither intelligent nor unintelligent/Not very intelligent/Not at all intelligent/Don't know?' One response to such a survey might be that if you ask a stupid question, you may well get a stupid answer. But let's accept that the surveys reflect an evaluative hierarchy in terms of accents. The question is, what does it mean? The salient point is surely that the significant evaluation being made is not of accents (accents can't be intelligent or trustworthy, since they don't have agency), but speakers. In other words, what such surveys indicate is a set of inculcated attitudes towards people who speak with the form of pronunciation belonging to the region and class into which they were born. After all, the surveys assess how words are spoken, not what is being said (the surveys don't give examples of actual speech), which amounts to nothing other than a form of prejudice. Indeed it is often said that linguistic prejudice, specifically 'accent prejudice', is the last 'socially acceptable' form of prejudice (a risible claim, given the other forms of prejudice in Britain that seem to be perfectly socially acceptable). But it's important to be clear what prejudice is: rather than some sort of idiosyncratic preference, it is an ingrained and usually unconscious way of categorizing people in negative and demeaning ways. In other words, it is deeply ideological and rooted in the exercise of power.

I have experienced linguistic prejudice during my education, as I have during my academic career (that surprised question, 'oh, what do you do at the university?', that surprised look when I say 'professor of English'). On two separate occasions, in two of the institutions in which I have worked, I have been asked by colleagues – linguists no less – if I can 'do Scouse'. And at another event, invited to speak at a major British university, I was introduced as someone with 'a pronounced Liverpool accent' (which is a very odd phrase indeed). None of which is entirely without precedent of course. After all, the tone was set by Henry Wyld, an important early historian of the English language (educated privately at Charterhouse and in Lausanne, and then at Corpus Christi, Oxford, he later became Professor of English Language at Liverpool before moving on to the Merton Professorship of English Language and Literature at Oxford). In *The Growth of English* (1907), Wyld observed that 'if we can truthfully say of a man that he has a Scotch accent, or a Liverpool accent, or a Welsh accent, or a London accent, or a Gloucestershire accent, then he does not speak "good English" with perfect purity' (Wyld 1907: 48). Like all forms of prejudice, linguistic prejudice is painful, obstructive, annoying, tedious, and potentially damaging; it is systematic, inscribed in institutions and disseminated in a variety of forms (ranging from abuse to so-called jokes) on a daily basis. But I cannot say that it has affected me unduly, not least because I have had the good fortune to acquire the cultural resources and confidence to deal with it, derived, in part, from my knowledge of the English language and its history. I am familiar with the sorry history of linguistic stigmatization that runs from the Renaissance to the present (very briefly sketched out above). I also know how variable the perception of linguistic forms can be: during the 1960s, the Liverpudlian accent was a prestige rather than stigmatized form (at least in popular culture). And I am also aware, from my time living in the United States, that people not brought up with the system of linguistic prejudice that runs through British social life do not evaluate British accents in the ways recorded in the linguistic attitude surveys. Indeed, my accent was once described by my students in California as 'posh' (I laughed). I understand too the social function that prejudicial views about language have: to naturalize social hierarchy and to inculcate deference and a sense of inferiority. And yet, although I am in a position to reject linguistic prejudice as tedious nonsense, as one of those traditions that does not deserve respect, I am also fully cognizant of the fact that it is imbricated in networks of social power whose aim and function is to exclude and diminish people, to deny them opportunities, to treat them unequally. The consequences of the historical process of elevating some forms of language, and deprecating others, are socially real and materially damaging. There will be many working-class women and men, some of whom I grew up with, who will have borne the weight of the type of ignorant, studied (Charterhouse, Oxford), social rudeness typified by Henry Wyld and his ilk.

The cultural effects of being told that your language is non/sub-standard, that it is in some sense always secondary, not quite good enough, are captured in a famous passage in James Joyce's *A Portrait of the Artist as a Young Man* (1916). It is part of an exchange between a young Irishman, Stephen

Dedalus, and an English Dean of Studies, in which Stephen uses a word – 'tundish' – which the Dean does not recognize (he uses its equivalent – 'funnel'). 'I never heard the word in my life', says the Dean, to which Stephen retorts that the word is used 'in Lower Drumcondra ... where they speak the best English'. Stephen laughs as he makes this reply, but he soon feels 'a smart of dejection' and is 'disheartened' and silent. He reflects on the lesson of the exchange:

> The language which we are speaking is his before it is mine. How different are the words *home, Christ, ale, master*, on his lips and on mine! I cannot speak or write these words without unrest of spirit. His language, so familiar and so foreign, will always be for me an acquired speech. I have not made or accepted its words. My voice holds them at bay. My soul frets in the shadow of his language. (Joyce 1992: 205)

Truth be told, Stephen's dejection changes to anger when he looks 'tundish' up (it was on his mind 'for a long time') and finds that it is 'English and good old blunt English too'. 'Damn the dean of studies', he exclaims, and concludes by asking, 'what did he come here for to teach us his own language or to learn it from us?' (Joyce 1992: 274).

The same sort of linguistic alienation is expressed in Una Marson's 'Little Brown Girl', a poem that adopts the voice of a racist in an encounter in London in the 1930s:

> You speak good English
> Little brown girl,
> How is it you speak
> English as though it belonged
> To you?
> (Marson 2011: 94)

I understand the sentiment that lies behind the words of Joyce and Marson (though it is important not to conflate experiences and to respect the differences of history – their experience is not mine). On the other hand, and perhaps for the reasons outlined above, I can't say that I've ever shared it. I've certainly come across this type of condescending attitude ('is that what you call it? I've never heard that before' – as though linguistic ignorance is something to boast about), but I've never felt intimidated by it. I was aware of the limitations of my own knowledge and experience, but I never suffered from 'impostor's syndrome' (not least because I realized relatively early on that there were more than a few impostors in university life at all levels – I just wasn't one of them). In any case, to return to Marson's poem, the answer to the racist's question is quite simple. How is it that any speaker of English uses the language 'as though' it belongs to them? Because it does.

Our common language

I wouldn't go as far as to claim that they speak 'the best English' in Liverpool – in the Dingle, say – partly because I don't think the category makes sense (what will count as a good use of language will depend on the context). On the other hand, Liverpool English is a living and developing, complex, and functional vernacular form of English that serves its speakers well. I choose to call it a vernacular for two reasons, First, because the term avoids the connotations of 'heritage' that attach to 'dialect' – a stance that lies deep within the roots of dialectology, though it is sustained by a number of professional and amateur organisations, for whom language is seemingly always something that was. And, second, because the etymology and semantic development of 'vernacular' – from *verna*, 'homeborn slave' to the later meaning of 'indigenous, domestic, native' – is suggestive. Rather than a dialect with fixed boundaries (the borders of language are porous – there is no claim in my work that the words of Liverpool English are exclusive to Liverpool – many of them aren't), Liverpool English is a form that has thrown off its putative bondage to 'the best'/'standard' English to become indigenous.

That is not to say that Liverpool English is always hailed by its users, since there is often an ambivalence in responses to 'Scouse' (not my preferred term) within the city. This is hardly surprising in one sense, given the consistent stigmatization of the form over a very long period of time in all sorts of different media. But, on the other hand, my own experience tells me that there is tremendous interest in the Liverpool vernacular in Liverpool. I give two examples. When I was a kid, I spent a lot of time in Garston library (at the top of Stormont Road, where my nan lived). It was a wonderful Carnegie library, with polished floors and a world of books. I had three treasured green cardboard tickets with my name, 'Anthony Crowley', and a number printed in red. I found it hard to believe that they would let me take the books home. My teacher, Miss Jacques (pronounced Jakes, as in Shakespeare's joke in *As You Like It* – 'Jacques'/'Jakes' – an early modern English term for 'toilet'), asked me once if I read the books I took out of the library. I had no idea what she meant (read as opposed to colour the pictures in?). Anyway, as a way of saying a small thank you to that library for the life-long debt that I owe it, when *Scouse: A Social and Cultural History* (Crowley 2012) appeared, I took a copy to donate to the collection. A lot of the book-space had been given over to computers for internet access and a 'one-stop shop' for jobs and benefits, and the opening hours were limited, but the library was there in all its wonder still. The librarian was pleased, but, she told me, 'we'll have to keep it on reserve because there'll be a lot of demand' (the words any author wants to hear). The second example, which testifies to interest in the language of Liverpool among its inhabitants, is furnished by the response to a series of talks around the city to promote *Scouse* and *The Liverpool*

English Dictionary (2017). Always engaged and funny and sometimes contentious ('that's not what that word means round here, mate'), those events were consistently illuminating and informative (at least from my perspective). One thing that those audiences taught me was that Liverpool has a large population of experts on language; 'imagine', as one of the city's more famous sons once sang.

Evidently, I share that interest in our 'common language', though that phrase is worth exploring, given that 'common' is one of those words that is often used to describe Liverpool English. Used in a pejorative sense, 'common' (as in 'talking common') is recorded from the fourteenth century with the sense of 'not distinguished by any special or superior quality; relating to or characteristic of ordinary people', though from the same period, it also means 'undistinguished by rank, position, wealth, etc.; of ordinary or low social status; belonging to the masses'. That social distinction – the common people rather than those of a higher class (which is what 'rank, position, wealth' mean) – takes on a negative cultural sense from the late eighteenth century on (when the modern British class system was constructed), as 'common' comes to mean 'lacking refinement; vulgar, coarse, low class'. And it is this meaning of course that people are using when they refer to 'common speech' or 'common language'. Needless to say, I reject that pejorative and disrespectful meaning. I am interested instead in the 'common language' of Liverpool, by which I mean a shared, public, open, communal ('common' is the root of 'community') language that was forged by people in history in a particular place over a distinct period of time. In this book, I have tried to show my appreciation of that vernacular form by approaching it from an innovative and, I hope, productive perspective. What I have not attempted to do in this work is to write an autobiography, or even an autobiographical account of part of my life (since, in truth, the text covers a specific period of personal and social history). Rather, I have tried to interweave my own experience of growing up in Liverpool (and of 'being from' Liverpool), with social history, and the history of words. By doing so, my intention is to show how – for any of us – our subjective life is shaped and influenced by the specific language that is a product of the situated history that both limits and liberates our social being: our common language set within our common history.

Note on offensive terms and methodology

Liverpool English, like all other forms of English, contains words that are offensive or derogatory in various ways. In keeping with the aims of this work, I have recorded these terms as evidence of a living language marked by the history in which it was produced and that it in turn shaped. Ignoring such terms would falsify social and linguistic history and therefore I have included them but treated them analytically – seeking to bring out their origins, development and use, while signaling the negative effects that they engender. In my accounts of the words taken for consideration in this text, I have attempted to apply the historical principles that inform the *Oxford English Dictionary* (*OED*) and indeed my own *Liverpool English Dictionary* (*LED*). If the reader comes across words with which they are unfamiliar, they are probably to be found in the *LED*, or its big brother, the *OED*.

In relation to methodology, I have adopted the following practice. I have selected an alphabetical format as a way of organizing the material. But rather than simply discussing the title word of each chapter, I have used that word as a starting point on a journey through personal, social and linguistic history. By doing so I have attempted to explore the complex, unpredictable but significant ways in which the web of language connects us to others in the past, present and future.

ACE

'Ace' was the word. Its force has weakened now to make it a slightly stronger version of 'cool' (often signaling no more than agreement or acceptance); but when kids wanted to express extreme approval, 'ace' was our word. 'That is just ace': there was no higher expression of enthusiasm. 'Ace' has a peculiar history though, since its earliest meaning was 'bad luck, misfortune, nothingness', as in Chaucer's *The Monk's Tale* (1405): 'The sys [six] Fortune hath turned into an aas' (Chaucer 1988: 250). This sense derived from the use of the term to refer to the side of a dice with a single spot (the lowest number) and has its origin in the Latin *as*, a unit of measurement. By the sixteenth century, the meaning had shifted to mean either the highest or lowest value, because of the role of the ace in card games. This led in turn, through a process of semantic amelioration, to the early twentieth-century appearance of the adjectival sense of 'ace', meaning 'excellent' (and 'ace' as a non-specific name for an admirable person). Semantic reversals of this kind are not unusual in the history of English. An example of a word that has suffered semantic degeneration (as opposed to the semantic amelioration of 'ace') is 'bully', which was originally a term of endearment for a companion or friend, as in *Henry V*: 'from my heart strings I love the lovely bully' (Shakespeare 1974: IV i 49).

The coinage of the twentieth-century adjectival sense of 'ace' is classed as an 'Americanism' (a word whose history was briefly touched upon in the Introduction). In the late eighteenth century, the declaration of American political independence was accompanied by calls for a concomitant form of linguistic autonomy, typified by Noah Webster's call for Americans to 'seize the moment, and establish a *national language* as well as a national government' (Webster 1789: 406). Webster played his part in that process by compiling a dictionary of American English – the *American Dictionary of the English Language* (1828) – which popularized American spellings such as 'color', 'center' and so on. This revolt against British cultural standards (accompanied by developing economic rivalry) provoked anti-American sentiment in Britain, including condescending or pejorative attitudes towards 'Americanisms', and it reflected the hardening links between the English language and a particular type of English identity that developed from the eighteenth century on. In fact, linguistic anti-Americanism persists as a general attitude, often in the form of a type of English cultural snobbery. I heard it frequently at Oxford; I used 'itemize' in an essay once, and it was met with open scorn (my tutor told me that it was 'not a word'). But, in truth, such objections are usually based on misconceptions or ignorance. In the First Folio of Shakespeare's works, for example, 'color' and 'center' are commonly used. And 'sidewalk', a word that can provoke the rolling of eyes in Britain, was originally, to use James Joyce's phrase that I cited earlier, 'English and good old blunt English too'; it was loaned to America in the eighteenth century. In fact, 'sidewalk' is retained in Liverpool English in the contraction 'side', meaning pavement. Indeed, the evidence shows that while linguistic anti-Americanism may have been significant generally in British culture, that was not the case in Liverpool: American English was one of the most important historical influences in the formation of the city's vernacular. From a personal point of view, I gained an insight into the linguistic creativity of American English while teaching in the United States. Discussing word formation, specifically the creation of verbs from nouns, I asked if anyone could think of an example. 'To nounize', came the confident reply.

Liverpool's role as a conduit for American English, as well as American fashion and, crucially, music, is explained by the fact that it was the main British transatlantic port from the mid eighteenth century (starting with its involvement in the slave trade). The influence of American culture on Liverpool life in the past couple of centuries or so has often been under-estimated. But Liverpool's role in transatlantic trade and political relations from the early nineteenth century could hardly be exaggerated (Herman Melville's *Redburn*, published in 1849, gives an account of the fascination that Liverpool held for at least one young American). A sign of the city's significance was that it hosted a United States Consulate, considered to be a prestigious diplomatic position (Nathaniel Hawthorne, author of *The Scarlet Letter*, published in 1850, held the post between 1853 and 1857 – he hated it). More importantly, from the early nineteenth century on, the extent of the Atlantic trade entailed not simply a prodigious circulation of goods between Liverpool and cities such as Boston and New York, but also a constant flow of people and thus culture and language. Cotton may have been the mainstay of the trade, but words, often brought and popularized by 'Cunard Yanks' (Liverpool seamen staffing the transatlantic routes), were an important by-product. The general point was made by Frank Shaw, despite his reductive and highly popular account of the origins of 'Scouse' (see the entry under **Scouse**): 'The lingo [of Liverpool] is a palimpsest of speech habits and slang from all over the world, imported by the much-travelled natives of Merseyside, and especially from the United States, with which the port had close contact before any other port in the country' (Shaw 1955: 18).

There are many words other than 'ace' that demonstrate the extent to which American English shaped Liverpool

English. 'Boss' as a familiar but polite term of address (my father regularly called strangers either 'boss' or 'chief'), and the more recent 'boss' in the sense of 'brilliant, wonderful', are both American borrowings (originally from the Dutch *baas*, 'master', originally 'uncle'). Likewise, the strong Liverpool term 'bad news', in the sense of 'something seriously bad, unacceptable, dangerous'; in American English it originally meant a 'restaurant bill'. 'Black Maria', for police van, is a mid nineteenth-century Americanism (though the origin of 'Maria' is unknown), as is the related 'hurry-up van'. 'Bunk in'/'bunk on'/'bunk off', from around the same period, all probably derive from the American usage 'bunk', 'to cheat or deceive'. 'Nosh', 'to eat/food' is originally Yiddish *nashn*, 'eat a snack', but came via America. And 'to sweat on', in the sense of 'await anxiously' probably came from American gambling discourse via First World War Forces' slang (hence its entirely appropriate use in bingo parlours – my nan regularly sweated on one number, to her great chagrin).

'Slummy' and 'scally' are interesting Liverpudlian American words. 'Slummy', in the sense of slum-dweller, first appears in the title of Pat O'Mara's wonderful *Autobiography of a Liverpool Irish Slummy* (1934). But the more common Liverpudlian term 'slummy', meaning 'waste material' and, by extension, 'coppers, loose change', is from the early twentieth-century American term 'slum', 'fake or counterfeit jewelry', or 'worthless prize offered at a fair'. 'Scally', on the other hand, is a late twentieth-century Liverpool coinage whose meaning was originally relatively neutral or even, in context, positive. In the 1980s it referred to young working-class Liverpudlian men who were interested in football and fashion (I didn't qualify because I couldn't afford to be interested enough in clothes); the dress code was 'casual' (very precisely defined), constantly evolving, and strictly policed (wearing a scarf was a serious faux pas). 'Scally' soon pejorated, however, to its meaning of 'a young working-class person (esp. a man);

specifically, a roguish, self-assured male, typically regarded as boisterous, disruptive, or irresponsible' (*OED*). It thus returned semantically to its etymological origins in mid nineteenth-century American English: a good-for-nothing (in trade union discourse, someone who won't work), and later, a political ne'er-do-well, particularly a Southern white person who refused post-Civil War Reconstruction. 'Scally' is a harsh insult these days; it is often used with a sense of anti-social or criminal behaviour.

Work, not least dock work, was another discursive area that featured American imports. The 'sarnies' that dockers (and, by transfer, other workers) took to work were called 'carrying out', a term that derived from the American English 'carry out', meaning 'prepared food and drink for consumption away from the premises of sale' (now more commonly known as 'take-away'). While a 'growler' was a tin can used by dockers to keep their 'carrying out' fresh; it came specifically from New York and originally meant 'a container to carry home beer bought in a bar'. Staying with the docks, 'stevedore', an older usage than the related 'docker' (a late eighteenth-century coinage that originally referred to someone who lived near the docks), was an American borrowing from Spanish – *estivador*, from *estivar*, 'to stow cargo'. Yet the practical vocabulary of work was not the only field in which American usage exerted its influence. More than a few American words were incorporated into the Liverpudlian vernacular by way of popular culture, particularly through the 'pictures' (cinema), sometimes known as the 'flicks' (from 'to flicker'). 'Cowies' (cowboy films) brought 'vamoose' ('go away'), from the Spanish *vamos*, 'we go'/'let's go', and, one of my dad's favourites, 'skedaddle' (move off, escape). 'Skedaddle' is interesting in that its roots may be in Ancient Greek, σκεδάννῦμι, *skedánnumi* – 'scatter, disperse', but it seems to have existed in Scottish and Northern vernacular usage before being exported to America and then imported back through cowboy speech to the streets of Liverpool. 'Filums' (an Irish pronunciation that persists), most of which depicted gangsters, also brought 'poke', 'scratch' and 'spondulics' (all terms for money).

I was ambivalent towards America as a kid, culturally and politically. On the one hand it seemed to represent modernity, excitement, energy and opportunity – sentiments transmitted through various forms of popular culture – and it gave us the music to which we listened and danced, and the films that we imitated and mocked. On the other hand, it was brash, over-confident, brutally capitalist, and up to no good all over the world – even as a child I was aware of Vietnam and then, as a teenager, American involvement in the barbarity in South and Central America. I protested against Richard Nixon visiting the Oxford Union in my first year at Oxford and was punched by an American Secret Serviceman in St Michael's Street for my pains (it was the day before my eighteenth birthday). Despite boxing in the Irish Guards cadets on Windsor Street in the Dingle, where there were many much better boxers than me, I'd never been hit that hard; the British cop who picked me up said 'ouch' and sent me on my bemused way. Even so, I was surprised by the anti-American sentiment at the university, much of which, as noted above, was cultural snobbery of the most condescending sort, sometimes masquerading as political critique. I didn't share in it – cultural snobbery in that form really wasn't available to me as a stance – but it was pretty commonplace on the political left and right. Tories appeared to hate America out of some imperial angst (boy that Declaration of Independence still seemed to rankle – and I suppose if you think you should still have an empire, it makes sense to resent the new imperialists). Meanwhile, the student left, for the most part, had little knowledge of American history as far as I could see (I was lucky enough to come across Howard Zinn's powerful, if sometimes reductive, *People's History of the*

United States when it came out in 1980). Like the Tories, most of my left contemporaries saw capitalism, racism, the new empire, and nothing else in America – as though it had no socialist tradition, no proud history of struggle and resistance.

I inherited an openness towards America from my upbringing – my dad was fascinated by the place, and John Kennedy's inauguration speech hung on a wall at home. And, more broadly, references to American popular culture were hardly uncommon in Liverpool, as evinced by the 'Wild West Poems' of Adrian Henri, a Sound Mersey man:

1. Noon:

2. tall gunmen walking slowly towards each other down Mathew St ....

3. William H. Bonney alias Billy the Kid hitches his horse to a parkingmeter strides through the swing doors into yates Wine Lodge. Barmaids slowly back away from the counter. Drunks rush out into Charlotte Street. He drinks a glass of Aussie White and strides out, silent as he came. (Henri, McGough, Patten 1967: 42)

When I got the chance to spend the best part of a year in America in 1986 I grabbed it with both hands and packed my ambivalence in my suitcase. I arrived on January 15th at Kennedy airport (I'd never felt cold like it) and, two weeks later, the *Challenger* space shuttle exploded. Myth has it that millions watched it live, but they didn't – they saw it, as I did, endlessly repeated on TV; I stood outside a store on Fifth Avenue late on the day it happened, watching it with a crowd – it was the first time I'd heard anyone say 'Oh my God'. I fell in love with New York, particularly when the weather turned in March. The summer was spent walking the city; on gloriously hot and humid summer Saturdays I caught the A train to Battery Park and walked up to a diner on 125th Street in Harlem. It was an ambulatory education in eight hours, and I had ample opportunities to test my ambivalence (I saw paramedics walking away from a homeless man who had died in a shop doorway near the Rockefeller Center). I shared the experience with my dad when he came to stay for three weeks. Standing on the top of one of the towers of the World Trade Center, where we'd been to an exhibition on gold (he was interested in gold), he declared: 'it's everything I knew it would be; I dreamt it like this'. It was one of the happiest moments of my life. Later in my career, I spent a year teaching in San Diego, largely recovering from my dad's death, and another at a research centre (center?) in Santa Cruz, which was one of the most important intellectual experiences of my life. And then I took the plunge and got a job at Scripps Colleges, one of the group of liberal arts colleges in Claremont California. I started in 2005, at the height of the Iraq war; 'welcome to the belly of the beast', the president of the college said as I arrived.

It was hardly that: Scripps had a small but beautiful campus and Claremont was a very liberal college town (in both respects it was completely un-American). It was situated at the foot of the San Gabriel mountains (snow-topped in the winter), and an hour from the beach and the high desert. It was hot to very hot throughout the year and I loved the flora and fauna the climate had produced. When our kids came along, I became an American citizen (dual with Britain) and, doing so, confirmed my constitutional place – which I've inhabited for most of my adult life – as an insider/outsider, participant/observer. Perhaps we all inhabit that space in various ways. In any case, I retained that status (along with my ambivalence) when I came back to Britain to work in academia.

I never did hear an American say 'spondulics', and I could never quite bring myself to say 'awesome' either (originally a term of serious force – usually applied to God). To my great joy, however, towards the end of my time in the States, I met an admirable man, the husband of our wonderful child minder. His name? What else but 'Ace'.

BOMMIE

'Remember, Remember the Fifth of November ...'. That admonition was wasted on us: we were well ahead of the game. Bommie night may have been in November, but for us it started in early September, at the end of the school holidays. Collecting the wood that is – the Guys came later (the timing of taking the Guys out was tricky: too early and there was great disapproval and no chance of any 'spare coppers'; too late and there was a Guy on every corner). 'Any old wood, mister?' We knocked on door after door of the terraced streets that surrounded the debby, also known as the oller; we were sometimes welcomed, often chased. It was surprising what we were offered. At one house down our street – Prophet Street, off Northumberland Street in the Dingle – the man came to the door and filled it; he seemed like a tired giant in dirty old work clothes. 'Round the back,' he ordered, and we walked around to the jigger, not entirely sure if we should go. But there he was, beckoning us, impatiently, so up the entry we went. We squeezed into the back yard, three of us, the oldest six years old, and there they were: a piano and two horsehair double mattresses. 'Can you take it?' There was a pause while we stared at it. 'Well?', he said. 'Ace,' our leader replied, 'but we need help – I'll get the others.' The excitement as we ran back to tell the big lads was palpable. 'A piano and two mattresses,' I shouted heroically; I was almost knocked down in the whooping rush. There's a lot of wood in a piano; I know that because we knocked it to bits in the entry – it was miles too big and heavy for us to carry in one piece. The intricacy of the keys fascinated me – so many articulate tiny pieces of good, dry (the essential detail) wood. The mattresses were heavy too and could only be dragged; they were dirty, smelly and damp from being in the backyard, but their horsehair insides burned furiously once you got them going.

Bonfires had their origins in violence and death; 'bonfire', as the *OED* has it, is 'an open-air fire for the public burning of heretics, proscribed books, etc' (I wonder what that 'etc' is meant to cover?). But Bonfire Night commemorates the plot to blow up King James I in 1605. Led by Guy Fawkes, the last man to enter parliament with honest intentions as anarchists say (a description that delighted my dad), the failure of the plot was followed by the torture of the conspirators and their dreadful executions. All apart from Guy, that is, who thwarted the aim of quartering him by falling off the scaffold and breaking his own neck (a rebel till the end). A priest once denounced bommie night, from the pulpit at St Patricks (our local church), as an anti-Catholic abomination; my dad, as faithful a Catholic as you could wish to meet this side of the laity, told us to 'take no notice of the old fool'. So we didn't, and we watched as Guy burned at last as he sat atop the fire in his scruffy rags and funny black hat (Welsh we thought). I often wondered where the word 'bonfire' came from; 'French – *bon feu*, good fire' my best mate at school, Tom, told me. And there it was, etymologically settled for many a year, until I looked it up (it pays to do the research). It's a medieval word, apparently coined to mark the striking of fires for St John's Eve (June 23rd); three fires were lit, one 'of clean bones and no wood'. Hence 'bonfire': 'a fire of bones, usually lit at midsummer'.

We built the bommie on the 'debby', or 'oller', or 'bombdie' – a large patch of empty ground that lay between Prophet Street, Fernie Street, and St Winefrides Honour School for Girls (a Catholic secondary school whose construction was greatly opposed by the local Orange Order). 'Debby' was from 'débris', 'oller' from 'hollow', 'bombdie' from 'bombed place', all references to the fact that inner-city Liverpool was pocked by clearances – patches of grimy, dusty wasteland – left by the bombing during the Second World War. These gaps (hollows), where streets once stood, were full of rubble (débris), the remnants of houses, pubs and shops. The streets that survived were themselves demolished in the 1970s (they were built in the 1850s and lacked indoor bathrooms and toilets), the city council completing the work that the Luftwaffe had begun. Unconscious of the irony of it, we played war on the debby, with the aim of defending our territory and, particularly, our wood. Given that wood collecting started months beforehand, this was a prolonged campaign and required a defensible shelter, a rotation of watchers, and enough ammo to repel enemies who included kids from streets the other side of Mill Street, the coggy watchman of St Winefrides, and council workmen. The dangers were clear; I stood on a rusty nail, an aerosol can exploded like a missile out of one of our small daily bonfires (we burned a lot of material), and Fat Charlie Mac had his head split open by a stone during a raid. Like all wars, the comradeship lasted; many years later, in town, I found myself staring at a face I knew but couldn't place. He came over: 'Alright To' (the shortened version of my name isn't a liberty in Liverpool, it's a norm), he said, putting out his hand: 'you don't recognize me, do you? Fat Charlie Mac'. Fat? He looked more like a body-builder who spent an inordinate amount of time in the gym to me. He delighted in showing me the scar on his head. Our glorious wounded.

'Guy' in the sense of 'man' (and more recently, in the plural, 'people' in general without any reference to gender) is an American import and a curious example of semantic widening (from Guy Fawkes to person of ugly appearance to ... just people). But that wasn't what we meant when we shouted 'Penny for the Guy', 'slummy for the Guy', outside The Farmers Arms, The Globe, The Warwick, or any of the myriad pubs on Park Road (experience demonstrating that adults with a few drinks inside them would the more easily part with their money). The Guy was a stuffed figure dressed in ill-fitting rags, though some kids used large dolls (which was considered cheating by the initiate); a pram was a bonus as it enabled you to move easily from spot to spot if you weren't making anything. Friday nights were favourite (people were paid in cash on Fridays) and, once the pennies had been gathered and divvied up, the calculation could begin as to how many 'bangers' could be bought in the morning. 'Astra bangers' they were, in thin purple tubes bearing the moniker 'ATOM'. We only bought 'bangers', and shops sold them as 'loosies' (singles) for 2d each. There didn't appear to be any age restriction, whatever it said on the shop door; indeed, as far as I could tell, they seemed to be bought exclusively by under-eighteens. I loved bangers and they stimulated my still far from repressed pyrotechnic tendencies ('pyrotechnic', interestingly enough, enters the English language in the early seventeenth century – not doubt old Guy had something to do with it – and it featured in a wonderfully titled treatise, *Pyrotechnia or a Discourse of Artificiall Fireworkes for Pleasure*, published in 1635). Light, smoulder, smoke, smell, sizzle ... BANG. Bangers worked best in jiggers – the confined space made the sound redound. To our repeated disappointment, they didn't work particularly well at all when you emptied all the gunpowder out of a few of them and made it into a small pile with a thin black fuse trail leading away. When you lit the fuse the flame scampered up to the pile, which then erupted in a loud ... PUFF. None of us understood the need to confine the potassium nitrate within a container; no box, no bang. My dad bought fireworks, which we watched in the back yard. 'Light up the sky with Standards Fireworks': 'Mine of Serpents', 'Jack-in-the-Box', 'Snow Storm',

'Shimmering Cascade', 'Catherine Wheel'. We hunted for the remnants the next morning and, ending our pyrotechnic adventures for another year, burned them.

I loved the smell that seemed to begin in October: the smoke from the combination of the coal that heated our houses and the constant fireworks. Looking down Northumberland Street towards the Mersey, with Cammell Laird shipbuilders on the other side, you could see the smoke mingling with the fogs that came off the river as the crepuscular streetlamps started to light up. It seemed magical and full of danger, which in truth it probably was given the levels of pollution in the air. Building bonfires in the middle of streets (which was common in the Dickens Streets on the other side of Park Road) was perilous too. But there is no denying the sense of autonomy and pride that was lost when the Corpy started to appropriate bommie night, first by arranging its own firework display in the city's parks, and then when it began to take all the wood away from local areas (fiercely resisted at first, the lorries just kept coming back). You could trace a social history of the powers of the state around Bonfire Night – from public executions to banning us from organizing our own bonfires.

November 5th was the main event, but there was another occasion for a bommie, though it took place in the early morning rather than night. On Good Friday, we burned Judas Iscariot (etymologically, the man from Kerioth) on the waste ground at the junction of Prophet and Fernie Streets. There were no fireworks at that time of year, but there was an effigy of Judas Carry-out, as we called him. Like Guy, Judas was the means by which small change was begged in the days of Holy Week: 'Judas, Judas, penny short of his breakfast'. Though very early, the tween of twilight mediated by the ubiquitous smoky haze, I was allowed to go to the bonfire. Perhaps because I was so young, I thought that everyone burned Judas on Good Friday morning. It turned out that it was a very local practice, mostly restricted to the docklands in the south of the city, around Park Road and Mill Street. Where did it originate? That is an anthropological mystery, though the likelihood is that sailors from the Mediterranean (where it was widely performed in Spain, Portugal and Greece) brought it as a cultural custom in the nineteenth century and it stuck – a bit like that Portuguese fish-on-Friday speciality, Bacalhoa, or salt fish. Was it anti-Semitic? I'm not sure. It may simply have been a scapegoating ritual, akin to burning the Guy, or Haman during Purim (at least in older Jewish traditions). But although, at one level, Guy and Judas may simply have represented the narrative figure of the betrayer who needs to be expelled, these practices are hardly empty of content. After all, it isn't as though the deep historical discourses of sectarianism and anti-Semitism have disappeared. Unwitting as it was, we may have been stoking very old flames as we built and burnt those bommies.

CASH

'Cash' appeared in English in the late sixteenth century to mean a 'chest or box for money' (from the French *case*, modern French *caisse*, ultimately Latin *capsa*), but the development of the metaphorical general sense of 'money' was more or less contemporaneous. In 'Haue with you to Saffron-Walden' (1596) Thomas Nashe writes of a miser: 'he put his hand in his pocket but to scrub his arme a little that itcht, and not to pluck out anie cash' (Nashe 1883: III 133). There wasn't much cash in my dad's pockets; he brought up five children, with seven years between them, as a single parent on a working-class wage (my mother left in the late 1960s when my youngest sibling was three). From time to time I read with annoyed astonishment those nostalgic accounts that make it seem as though poverty was not something that its victims noticed (as though we were oblivious to other worlds), or that being poor was fine because we were happy (as if social solidarity was the same as the ease furnished by material comfort), or that we were all in it together (as though there were no differences between us). Being poor meant that we couldn't do things, own things, go places; as children we were aware of that – how could we not be? We knew that we were in it together, but very conscious of the fact that we weren't 'all in it together' (that, as we have all learned, was just another Tory slogan). That lingering smart of dejection associated with the limitations placed on us doesn't fade. And being excluded socially on a systematic basis marks you psychically – how could it not? I remember pretending not to want to go to town with friends because there wasn't the money; feigning indifference to fashionable clothes, nice holidays, a colour TV, central heating ... I dissembled because what else was there to do? Being poor was bad enough; owning it was something else altogether.

My dad had no fear of debt, as far as I could tell, although who knows how much it nagged at him in the lonely hours of the night. He certainly gave the impression of not caring, of being unafraid of authority and its pressing demands. We did skip prize day once, because, as I learned later, the chair of the board of governors was a local magistrate, before whom my dad had appeared on number of occasions on debt summonses. 'I didn't want to embarrass us' was his comment. I thought at the time he meant me and my brother, though he could well have been referring to himself and the 'beak' (judge or magistrate). His lack of fear about money was an enormous strength on his part; it was double-edged for me. On the one hand, it meant that we were clothed and fed and looked after as well as he could afford: if my dad had money, he spent it, usually on us ... if he didn't have money, he spent it anyway. On the other hand, I worried about the possibility of being taken into care (who would trust a single man to bring up five children?); I fretted over the threatening letters from the council; I was angry when the gas was disconnected; I was scared when we hid from debt-collectors; I hated bailiffs – they hunted in pairs (for their own safety probably), big men in Crombie overcoats – and I was resentful when, failing all else, my dad invited them in, gave them a drink, and made a token payment. 'Just doing their job', he used to say cheerily, to which of course came the predictable response from his teenage children about Nazis and concentration camp guards. When I went to university, we didn't have a phone at home because it had been cut off; my dad phoned me from a phone-box on Danefield Road at six sharp on Friday evenings – if we missed each other, he rang the next week. At the end of my first year I had money left over from the maintenance grant awarded to me by Liverpool Local Education Authority, and my dad borrowed it to reconnect the phone. A lesson in social investment you could call it.

'Don't worry about it', was my dad's laughing response to a lack of money. But I did worry about it, and I was aware of its power. I didn't need to read *Timon of Athens* to understand the potency of 'yellow, glittering, precious gold':

> Thus much of this will make
> Black white, foul fair, wrong right,
> Base noble, old young, coward valiant.
> Ha, you gods! Why this? What this, you gods? Why, this
> Will lug your priests and servants from your sides,
> Pluck stout men's pillows from below their heads.
> This yellow slave
> Will knit and break religions, bless th' accursed,
> Make the hoar leprosy adored, place thieves
> And give them title, knee, and approbation
> With senators on the bench. (Shakespeare 1974: IV
> iii 28–38)

Marx cites those lines in his account of 'the inverted world' of money, 'the confusion and exchange of natural and human qualities': 'it transforms loyalty into treason, love into hate, hate into love, virtue into vice, vice into virtue, servant into master, master into servant, nonsense into reason and reason into nonsense' (Marx 1975: 378–9). In this upside-down world, if you can afford to buy bravery, you're brave, even though you're a coward; likewise, intelligence if you're stupid, social skills if you're gormless, honesty if you're a crook, popularity if you're an outcast. My father didn't need money to buy those things; he needed it to keep the house warm, the lights on, clothes on our backs. When I was twenty-seven, I took on more debt than my father could ever have accessed when I bought a flat. I was told by the estate agent to think of it as 'a good investment of capital', rather than, as she could have said, a home; another example of the 'distorting and confounding' nature of money.

There has always been an alternative discourse of finance and, in Liverpool, there was a whole set of general words for money apart from 'cash': 'boodle' (an Americanism used in the city in the early twentieth century, ultimately from the Dutch *boedel*, 'estate, possessions, inheritance'); 'dosh' (etymology unknown); 'poke' (from Old French *poche*, 'bag' [compare 'pouch'], later 'wallet' or 'purse'); 'readies' (a modern version of the seventeenth-century 'ready', short for the earlier phrase 'ready money'); 'splosh' (etymology unclear, possibly from 'splash', as in 'splash out'); 'sponduliks' (etymology unclear, possibly related to the Greek σπνδή, *spondé* – 'offering of wine to the Gods', 'solemn drink offering on the occasion of a truce', hence 'payment, fee, gratuity'). My own experience of the language of money was conditioned by one of those extremely rare events in the history of a society – a change in the monetary system itself (known to us as the shift from 'old money' to 'new money'). There was a Liverpudlian aspect to this process: as well as topping the charts with 'Lily the Pink', The Scaffold (Mike McCartney, who was the brother of the slightly more famous Paul, John Gorman and Roger McGough) sang ditties for the public information films that heralded the introduction of decimalization on February 15th, 1971. The refrains seemed like injunctions, which no doubt exacerbated the sense that the whole thing was a deceptive imposition: 'give more get change'; 'use your old coppers in sixpenny lots'; 'decimalization, decimalize, decimalization, decimaliiiiiize'. I was ten when this momentous event happened, which meant that the way I had learned to count money (twelve pennies to a shilling, twenty shillings in a pound, 240 pennies in a pound – which made for a lot of penny twists) had to be renounced and a new system learned all over again (no shillings and only 100 pennies to the pound – which seemed to me, and my nan, deeply suspicious – fewer penny twists for sure). I became pretty adept at calculating prices in 'new' and 'old money' for older people ('how much is 9½p?' – 'nearly two shillings, about nineteen pence' – 'for a loaf? The robbers!'). I used to challenge myself to convert prices as fast as possible ('77½p – fifteen and six', 'nine bob – 45p', '2½p – a tanner/ sixpence', 'twelve shillings – 60p'); this was a useful skill with which to impress my elders, particularly the gamblers among them. When I worked in a bookies in my teens, there were still some punters who wrote '5 bob @ 5–1' on their betting slips. On the few occasions that they won, Josie Jennings, the bookie, wrote the winnings as '£1–10 shillings settled' (5 x 25p = £1.25 plus 25p stake = £1.50 as we would now say). 'Settled' was Josie's way of saying that she would brook no arguments about the calculation. People, rightly, used to contend with her about half a penny.

There had in fact been a complex Liverpudlian vocabulary for the elements and combinations that made up the old system of 'pounds, shillings and pence' (itself a general phrase meaning money). Many, though not all, of these words were already obsolete by the time I was born. They included (from the smallest up): 'fudge' (a late nineteenth-century term for a farthing – etymology unknown); 'brown' (a farthing or halfpenny – recorded from the early nineteenth century, presumably derived from the colour of the coins); 'mopus' (farthing or halfpenny – first recorded in the seventeenth century and perhaps from the German slang *möpse*, 'money'); 'meg' (halfpenny – possibly a corruption of the sixteenth-century cant 'make'); 'og' (halfpenny – perhaps a corruption of 'hog', a seventeenth-century term for a shilling, based on a picture of a pig on the coin, though this may be speculative); 'win' (penny – said to be an abbreviation of 'Winchester', though it's not clear why); 'dodger' (eight-sided three-penny bit – etymology unknown); 'joey' (the twelve-sided threepenny bit

– claimed to refer to Joseph Hume, the MP who campaigned for its introduction); 'tiddler' (silver threepenny bit – probably from the sense of 'tiddler' as 'something small' – the fish in Sefton Park lake for example); 'spraza'/'sprowser' (sixpence, sixpenny piece – though the etymology is unclear, it is probably from the Romani and Shelta terms for 'sixpence' – *spars, sprazi*); 'tanner' (sixpence – an eighteenth-century word, possibly derived from the Romani *tanna*, 'small'); 'bob' (a shilling, plural 'bob', as in 'two bob' – etymology unknown, though it appeared to alternate in the early nineteenth century with 'bobstick'); 'levy' (a shilling – an early nineteenth-century Americanism imported to Liverpool, etymology unclear); 'ocker' (one shilling – etymology possibly related to Old English *oker*, 'lending money'); 'half a dollar' (two shillings and sixpence); 'tusheroon' (two and six – recorded from the mid nineteenth century, though the etymology is unclear); 'dollar' (five shillings – though the coin was officially the 'crown', the use of 'dollar' probably derived from the period when the pound was worth four dollars, as it was under the gold standard between 1817 and 1931); 'half-bar' (ten shillings); 'half a nicker' (ten shillings); 'bar' (a pound – defined in Samuel Johnson's *A Dictionary of the English Language* (1755) with reference to colonialism – 'a denomination of price; payment being formerly made to the Negroes almost wholly in iron bars', though more likely to be from the Romani *bar*, 'pound, money and weight'); 'nicker' (a pound – plural 'nicker', as in 'ten nicker', ten pounds – the term dates from the mid to late nineteenth century, and may belong to racing slang, though the etymology is unclear); 'deuce' (two pounds – from the French *deux*); 'bluey' (five pound note – the name derived from the introduction of the dark blue five pound note as a replacement for the 'white fiver' in 1957); the basis of 'fiver', 'tenner', 'twenty' and so on is clear enough.

Apart from its most common and general meaning, the term 'money' itself had a specific sense: 'wages' or 'pay'. This usually appeared in a variety of evaluative phrases: 'good money' (satisfactory wages); 'not bad money' (adequate pay); 'poor/rubbish/crap money' (inadequate renumeration, which could also be referred to disparagingly as 'coppers'). If you had money, you might be 'tapped' ('to tap' was 'to ask for a loan' – appropriately enough the derivation seems to be from 'to tap' as 'insert a tap to draw liquor from a cask') for a 'sub' (an abbreviation of a mid nineteenth-century coinage, a 'subsist', itself a shortening of 'subsistence money', the 'payment of wages on account'). If you didn't have money, you'd inform the person asking that you were 'skint' (early twentieth-century Forces' slang, probably from 'skinned') or 'brassic' (rhyming slang – 'boracic lint', 'skint'). Being skint was a widespread, unfortunate and much-lamented condition. It was a puzzle to me to try to imagine who wasn't skint.

I had an overwhelming childhood sense that there never was and never would be enough cash. That mattered in Liverpool, where having 'a few bob' in your pocket was important. But there were other lessons that I picked up. For example, as noted above, the perception that 'old money' was more reliable, trustworthy and, hence, valuable than the 'new money' (a sense that is retained when people use a phrase of contemporary bureaucratic jargon and then translate it – as in 'downsizing the workforce – or sacking people, in old money'). I also came to realize that there was a mysterious time – 'then' – when all and any amount was 'a lot of money' (as in 'it cost a penny/sixpence/ten shillings/five pounds/one hundred pounds/a thousand pounds etc – which was a lot of money then'). But the most significant lessons that I learnt about money, from my father directly, were that the value of money is the good that you do with it, and that money only matters if you don't have any. Needless to say, the less you have, the more it matters.

DEKKO

Richard Verstegan's *Restitution of Decayed Intelligence in Antiquities concerning the most noble and renowned English Nation* (1605) is an important early account of the history of the English language. In the text, Verstegan defended the language against the charge that it was 'no language at all, but the scum of many languages', and railed against the importation of words (particularly Latin words, or words derived from Latin in the Romance languages) into English:

> For mine own part, I hold them deceived that think our speech bettered by the abundance of our daily borrowed words, for they being of another nature and not originally belonging to our language, do not, neither can they in our tongue, bear their natural and true derivation; and therefore as well may we fetch words from the *Ethiopians*, or East or West *Indians*, and thrust them into our language and baptise all by the name of English, as those which we daily take from the Latin, or the languages thereon depending. (Verstegan 1605: 204)

The basis of Verstegan's argument against word borrowing – that we might as well borrow words from Africa, the West Indies or India as from Latin – is historically ironic. *Restitution* was published at the very moment when the English nation state was in the initial stages of its imperial and colonial project, a historical development that had a considerable impact on the English language. An illustrative example is the word 'curry'; when people guess when 'curry' entered the language, the most frequent response is 'mid to late twentieth century' (presumably based on a misperception of multicultural Britain as a relatively recent development). In fact, 'curry' appeared in English in 1598, in van Linschoten's *Discours of voyages into ye Easte & West Indies*: 'somewhat sowre ... but it tasteth well, and is called Carriil'. It was borrowed from one of the world's oldest classical languages, Tamil, a language of south-east India: *kari*, 'sauce, relish for rice'. To coin a phrase, 'curry' is here because we were there.

Words travel in space and time, but their transmission is historical. Which is to say that words don't simply float freely across continents and centuries; they are carried by human beings and used in myriad practical activities. Word journeys can be short and direct, or they can be long, ranging over thousands of miles, with their arrival in any particular language mediated through other languages. Take that very common word 'dekko', for example, which I used as a child (and continue to use) in everday sentences such as 'give us a dekko', meaning 'let me have a look'. 'Dekko' (or 'decko'), is Hindi in origin, from *dekho* ('look!'), the imperative of *dekhnā*, 'to look'. It is first recorded in English in the late nineteenth century, though it appears as 'deck', 'look', slightly earlier in what the *OED* calls 'Anglo-Indian' (better known today as Indian English – note the shift of emphasis produced by the name change). The question is: how did a word from Hindi, an Indo-Aryan language spoken in India, find its way to the everyday speech of the streets of Liverpool?

To answer this question, it helps to remember that there are a good number of words in common Liverpool parlance that have travelled a long way from their origins. 'Ackers', for example, was one of the multitude of words for money; it probably derived from Egyptian Arabic *fakka*, 'small change', from *fakk*, 'to change money' (the Liverpool term for 'small change' is 'slummy'). Likewise, 'baksheesh', a 'tip or bribe', is from the Persian *baḵšiš*, 'present, gratuity', from *baḵšīdan*, 'to give'. From the same root (rather than rhyming slang) came 'buckshee', 'free, extra surplus'. Teachers and older people used 'buck' ('don't give me any buck/old buck'), meaning 'cheek or impudence', from Hindi *bak/buk buk*, 'talk, conversation' and, by extension, 'boastful or bragging talk', hence 'cheek'. And 'cushty' or 'custy' was common for 'excellent, brilliant'; derived from British Romani *kushto*, 'good', its ultimate root is possibly Persian *ḵušī*, 'pleasure, convenience', by way of Urdu *ḵušī* or Hindi *khush*, 'pleasure' (this is probably also the root of 'cushy' in English). 'Shufti', sometimes used instead of 'dekko' to mean 'look', came from the Arabic *šufti*, 'have you seen?', from *šāf*, 'to see', while 'yimkin', only used by the older generation in my recall, originally meant 'perhaps' in English, but by extension 'nonsense, rubbish' in Liverpool English; it derives from Iraqi Arabic *yimkin*, 'it may be'.

None of these words belong to Liverpool English exclusively, but some of them they did form part of my childhood vocabulary. As noted earlier, the interesting question is why words from languages used in India, Egypt, Persia (as was – now Iran), Iraq, and so on, ended up in the mouths of Liverpool schoolchildren? The fact is that these 'daily borrowed words', as Verstegan calls them, were brought by colonialism and war, since they are all originally recorded as part of what the *OED* calls 'Services' slang' or 'Military slang' – in other words, the everyday vernacular of British soldiers and sailors primarily. In truth, war is greatly underestimated as a motor of linguistic innovation and change in modern English. This is somewhat surprising given that, since the mid nineteenth century, Britain's major wars have involved the gathering of large numbers of (mostly) working-class men, from different regions of Britain, and their mobilization to places all around the globe. Indeed it would be more surprising if that process had not had an impact on English in all sorts of ways. For example, one effect of the mixing of large numbers of men from all over Britain would have been an awareness of linguistic difference, lexical and phonetic, related to regionality and class (such knowledge would previously have been relatively unusual). Another would have been the transmission of local words across Britain through adoption and use. Be that as it may, the question remains – how did words that came into English through military vernacular usage pass into Liverpool speech specifically? The answer lies in the fact that as well as being one of the world's great trading ports from the late eighteenth century, Liverpool was also an important military staging post – again, it was known as 'the gateway to Empire' for good reason. And through that gateway passed millions of military personnel, bearing their language with them, some of which stuck. How did it stick? What precise factors meant that some words passed into Liverpool speech? In specific terms, we don't know, though in general terms, we can say that the words that stuck and lasted must have been practically useful. If they hadn't had a use, then they would have faded from the living language. In that case they would have joined that myriad of dead words and meanings that the *OED* records so lovingly and wonderfully with the gloss 'obsolete', or they would simply have disappeared without trace.

The very fact that 'dekko' and all formed part of our everyday speech is evidence that linguistic borders are porous – if they weren't, there wouldn't be English words in languages across the world. That isn't to say, however, that there aren't determined efforts to police the boundaries. As noted above, in the Renaissance period, Verstegan rejected word borrowing on the basis that certain words are 'of another nature and not originally belonging to our language'. His attack was, however, slightly undermined when he cited an unnamed critic's observation that 'if we were to put to repay our borrowed speech back again, to the languages that may claim unto it; we shall be left little better than dumb' (Verstegan 1605: 204). It's a good point: take the 'foreign' words out of English, and what's left? Nonetheless, the desire to patrol the boundaries of English persisted (and persists). In *The Plan of a Dictionary of the English Language* (1747), the first great English dictionary, Samuel Johnson raised the difficulty that faces all lexicographers: 'it was not easy to determine by what rule of distinction the words of this dictionary were to be chosen'. The aim of the dictionary revealed the complexity of the enterprise:

> the chief intent of it is to preserve the purity and ascertain the meaning of our English idiom; and this seems to require nothing more than that our language be considered so far as it is our own; that the words and phrases used in the general intercourse of life, or found in the works of those whom we commonly style polite writers, be selected, without including the terms of particular professions; since, with the arts to which they relate, they are generally derived from other nations, and are very often the same in all the languages of this part of the world. (Johnson 1747: 4–5).

The demarcation of the language 'so far as it is our own' depended on a number of imprecise though significant exclusions: only the language of 'the general intercourse of life', of 'polite writers', and not 'the terms of particular professions ... derived from other nations'. And yet, as Johnson immediately conceded, the need for the dictionary to be useful required that the prohibition against 'foreign words' had to be reconsidered. They were, however, treated with caution, since 'all are not equally to be considered as parts of our language, for some of them are naturalised and incorporated, but others still continue aliens, and are rather auxiliaries than subjects' (Johnson 1747: 6). It is telling that Johnson uses the language of citizenship here, for although words are the immediate topic, larger questions of belonging and exclusion are always at stake in language debates. Of course the real question in such matters is where authority lies or, as Johnson himself put it, 'who shall judge the judges?'

(a version of Juvenal's question 'quis custodiet ipsos custodes', 'who guards the guards?'). Or as they say in Liverpool, 'says who?'

Prescribing 'foreign words' is not the only mode of policing the borders of language. There are those, for example, who Canute-like, make a stand against developments in meaning as the tide of linguistic change gradually, and sometimes not so gradually, flows over them (poor old King Cnut – the popular account is the exact reverse of what he was aiming to show by commanding the tide not to come in). '"Decimate" does not mean "to destroy"', I was once confidently and condescendingly told. 'What does it mean?', I asked (I was genuinely interested). 'To kill one in every ten', came the answer, 'from *decem*, the Latin for "ten"' (it's actually *decimus*, 'tenth', as in 'decimal', but there you go). 'We don't seem to have much need for a verb meaning "to kill every tenth one"', I replied; 'well that's what it means!', came the put down. On another, more recent, occasion I was informed by a colleague that '"inundate" doesn't mean "overwhelm"', because '"inundate" *really* means "to overflow"'. This is an amusing example, as it happens, and one that reveals the ignorance that lies behind such authoritarian posturing. *Undāre* does indeed mean 'to flow' in Latin, but in English the figurative sense of 'inundate' – to 'overwhelm, swamp' – predates the sense of 'flood' by more than a century and a half; one of the very earliest English dictionaries – Henry Cockeram's *English Dictionarie* (1623) – gives 'inundated' simply as 'overwhelmed'. In my experience, this sort of nonsense is actually often related to a type of lack of linguistic confidence, rather than assured knowledge, and it's frequently spouted by people with a smattering of Latin and less Greek (no trained Classicist could misunderstand the nature of linguistic change). None of which is to say that etymology is not absorbing – as will be clear from this work, I am fascinated by it. But my interest is not with the ἔτυμος, *étumos*, 'real, true', λόγος, *logos*, 'utterance, explanation, meaning', but with etymology as the tracing of the history of words as they change over time and in history. The 'origin' of a term is always significant (though of course 'origins' only go as far back as the written record – the history of writing imposes a limit), but it can't be given authority over what we do with our language. As the philosopher Ludwig Wittgenstein put it, 'the meaning of a word is its use in the language' (Wittgenstein 1967: ⁋43). Words mean what we use them to mean (which is why they are such notable markers of social change); they don't mean – by definition – what they used to mean, or what someone learned (or sometimes not so learned) in a classical language tells us that they mean.

A particularly harmful form of linguistic policing is the rejection of words because they are used by a specific group of people. Again, Johnson is a good example of this practice, as demonstrated in his defence of his exclusion of the language of 'the laborious and mercantile part of the people' (workers and traders) from his great *Dictionary* on the basis that,

> the diction is in a great measure casual and mutable; many of their terms are formed for some temporary or local convenience, and though current at certain times and places, are in others utterly unknown. This fugitive cant, which is always in a state of increase or decay, cannot be regarded as any part of the durable materials of a language, and therefore must be suffered to perish with other things unworthy of preservation. (Johnson 1755: Preface n.p.)

Behind most modes of prescriptivism, there is a desire to erase history, which comes in different forms. There is the rejection of word borrowing (this type of policing is currently out of fashion, though Americanisms still provoke annoyance – people used to get upset about 'hassle' before it became 'naturalized'). Another mode is found in resistance to linguistic change (this is enduringly popular – '"inundate" doesn't mean "overwhelm"!'). And there is the view that the language of some users of English is in some sense sub-standard and therefore not worth bothering with (this is a dominant belief – it is found in a range of fields as diverse as dialectology, literature and various forms of popular culture). The language I grew up in was that of the laborious part of the people (the working class we'd say nowadays). The polite way of demeaning it was to call it 'slang', though I've yet to meet anyone who can give a reasonable definition of that slippery term. The older definition of 'slang' in the *OED* is: 'the special vocabulary used by any set of persons of a low or disreputable character; language of a low and vulgar type'. The more recent version is: 'language of a highly colloquial type, considered as below the level of standard educated speech, and consisting either of new words or of current words employed in some special sense'. What I find interesting about this type of prescriptivism (the policing of language boundaries, a practice that often involves proscriptivism – the banning of language) is that it masquerades as descriptivism (an approach to language that purports simply to describe). I'm also struck by the ways in which the deceptive imprecision of these definitions allows them to exert social power. After all, what do the terms and phrases 'low', 'vulgar', 'colloquial', 'standard educated speech' mean? And where does 'dekko' (and the people who use the word) fit in such a pattern of categorization?

Rather than categorizing 'dekko' and words like it as slang, we could think of them in other terms. For given that language is a form of historical and political unconscious, we could say that 'dekko', 'akkers', 'baksheesh', 'buck', 'cushty'/'custy', 'shufti', 'yimkin' and all are radically (in the etymological sense of 'at root' – Latin *rādix*, 'root' – hence 'radish') the linguistic embodiment of colonial history. They are neither more nor less than the spoken reminders of a past that Britain prefers to forget, or, in the current mode of forgetting, revise.

EASY SIX

An 'easy six' is one of those expressions that mislead you. I knew what it meant as a kid, and I knew what it referred to – or at least I thought I did. As it turned out, although I understood its general meaning – 'a good or enjoyable time, an easy time of it' – I misunderstood its origin until I was in my forties. I thought it came from cricket – 'an easy six' being one of those soft balls tossed up to a batsman that they smashed out of the ground for six runs. In fact, it was a phrase taken from the discourse of dockers, which spread into general Liverpool use. An 'easy six' referred to the much-prized Sunday working on the docks, sought after because of the structure of the day (8–11am, 1–4pm) and the extra money that it brought. Frank Shaw illustrated the origin of the term when contrasting the old casual labour scheme of dock work with the more systematic organization that held by the late 1950s: 'What the young ones do not know, in these days of a guaranteed week, worked or not, and reasonable overtime pay (such as double pay, the Gold Nugget or the Easy Six), is how bad conditions once were' (Shaw 1959b: 6). Shaw exaggerated the extent to which the casual labour scheme (by which men queued up and were hired – or not – on a half-day basis) had disappeared by the late 1950s; decasualization started under the National Dock Labour Scheme of 1946, but it wasn't completed until 1967.

The history of dock building in Liverpool stretches back to the early eighteenth century, with the construction of the world's first enclosed commercial dock in 1715 (the

Old Dock). This was followed by Canning (1737), Salthouse (1773), Georges (1771), Dukes (1773), Kings (1785) and Coburg (1796–1972) docks. But it was in the mid to late nineteenth century that the great period of dock building occurred: Albert, Alexandra, Brocklebank, Brunswick, Canada, Clarence, Herculaneum, Hornby, Huskisson, Langton, Princes, Sandon, Stanley, Trafalgar, Victoria, Wapping and Waterloo docks were built on the Liverpool waterfront over a distance of seven and a half miles. And on the other side of the river, a further series was erected: Alfred, Bidston, Egerton, Great Float, Morpeth, Vittoria and Wallasey docks. The dock system struck one mid nineteenth-century observer, Herman Melville's Redburn, with awe:

> The sight of these mighty docks filled my young mind with wonder and delight ... In Liverpool, I beheld long China walls of masonry; vast piers of stone; and a succession of granite-rimmed docks, completely inclosed, and many of them communicating ... The extent and solidity of these structure, seemed equal to what I had read of the old Pyramids of Egypt ... In magnitude, cost, and durability, the docks of Liverpool, even at the present day surpass all others in the world. (Melville 1849: 204–5)

At their height in the 1950s, Liverpool docks employed some 25,000 dockers (on both sides of the Mersey); they were thus, by some distance, the city's largest employer. And it is perhaps for that reason that, as noted in the entry on **Mersey**, both the river and the docks that exploited it, were treated with a sort of reverence. In many ways, there was a sense that the docks captured something essential about Liverpool both as a location of work, but also in terms of the cultural identity of the city.

This was certainly true of the way in which the language of Liverpool was represented, and again the crucial figure in this regard was Frank Shaw, coiner of 'Scouse' to refer to Liverpool English and, among other roles, a customs officer on the docks. In an article in *The Liverpool Daily Post*, Shaw was cited as claiming that it was in Liverpool docks 'that Liverpool-ese was maintained and nourished to-day. Like other dialects it was dying; but it was nurtured in lusty health still by the dockers, who often keep themselves cut off from the world of the Oxford accent' ('Daily Post' Reporter 1955: 6). Despite the rather bizarre suggestion that dockers (deliberately?) isolated themselves from the pernicious influence of the 'Oxford accent' (a nonsensical if commonplace term), Shaw's claim for the docks as a special site of Liverpool language was reiterated in 'Strange Charm of the Lingo of Liverpool's Dockland', an article in *The Liverpool Echo* in 1959:

> Liverpoolese will never die as long as the port has dockers and it will be a long time before their skilled work can be wholly done by automation ... The lingo came from dockland in the first place ... It is dying in most parts of the city but still lives along Liverpool's thirty-eight miles of quay space. And those who hate uniformity will say let it live. (Shaw 1959b: 6)

Again, notwithstanding the horrible misjudgment of the effects of automation (or, more accurately, containerization) on employment, Shaw's observation strikes me as important for a number of reasons. It identifies the docks as the origin of Liverpool English; it proclaims the death of Liverpool English elsewhere in the city; it asserts that 'Liverpoolese' will be preserved as long as there are docks and dockers; and, finally, it proclaims that the maintenance of Liverpool English is a social good in that it will counter the effects of cultural uniformity.

What evidence is there to suggest that the docks were in fact a creative source of Liverpool English, or 'Scouse' as Shaw christened it in 1950? Apart from 'easy six', there is certainly some evidence to be found in the use of specific terms. Examples include: 'Blind O'Reilly' (an expletive), from a trade union activist on the docks in the early twentieth century; 'blocker', a bowler hat worn by foremen on the docks; the 'Bloody Forty', a criminal dock gang in the 1850s; 'cod boss', a foreman on the docks; 'day-old chick', new worker on the docks; 'in dock', in hospital, laid up; 'docker/docker's' (adjective), excessively big in size, as in 'docker butty'; 'docker's ABC', the typical conversation of dockworkers ('ale, baccy, cunt'); 'dockers umbrella', the Liverpool Overhead Railway; 'dockology'/'doxology' (the lore and language of dockers); 'fid', a marline spike, used in ropework; 'gold(en) nugget'/'nugget', weekend work on the docks that brought extra pay; 'growler', a tin for carrying sandwiches; 'to handball', to arrange cargo by hand; 'Harry Freeman's', something that is stolen or taken from the docks; 'hatches off', pub opening time; 'hook and book'/'on the hook and on the book' (phrase), a way of working and claiming unemployment benefit; 'Liverpool hook', a specific type of docker's hook; 'make up man', a supplementary member of a team; 'monkey-boat', a small tender or tow-boat used in the docks; 'nobber', a favoured worker in the casual labour system; 'not on' (adjectival phrase), unacceptable behaviour, probably from a reversal of 'on' when used to signal that a worker had been chosen under the casual labour scheme ('you're on, you're not on'); 'one o'clock gun', gun fired at one o'clock every day at Morpeth dock, Birkenhead, on a signal from Bidston Observatory, in order to keep accurate time; 'Paddy Kelly', dock policeman; 'Paddy Rileys', dock police force; 'pen'/'stand', an area where men queued for work under the casual labour scheme; 'putter on'/'taker on', man who selected workers under the casual labour scheme; 'the Rockery', the complex set of quays, locks and basins in Liverpool's seven miles of dock; 'scouseland', Liverpool; 'scouse shops', dockland cafes; 'to scow', to idle; 'sling your hook!, go away!' (if there was no work, a docker was told to 'sling your hook'); 'tally', a docket confirming work under casual labour system, or union membership;

'welt', unauthorized time-off. In addition to these lexical items, Shaw also cited dock nicknames as a sign of linguistic creativity: 'Just William', an elderly crane driver; 'the blood donor', a pale foreman; 'Happy Harry' and 'Mount Pleasant', a miserable soul (Shaw 1954: 4); 'Lino', someone perpetually short of money (on the floor); 'the Lenient Judge', a hatch foreman who calls to a crane driver, 'let her go'; 'Stanley Matthews', the skiver who takes the lightest end ('I'll take this corner'); 'Red Riding Hood', the man who lives with his granny (Shaw 1960b: 5). And so on, and so on.

From a linguistic point of view, this is interesting evidence, and it clearly shows that there was a relatively limited set of words created specifically at the docks. Yet does it demonstrate, as Shaw claimed, that the docks were both the origin and last bastion of Scouse? Two points need to be made. First, a distinction has to be made between 'dockland' and the 'docks' – 'dockland' referring to the working-class areas built around the waterfront in which the majority of Liverpool's population lived, and that served as the linguistic and cultural 'contact zone' in which 'Scouse' was forged. Shaw makes this distinction, but he doesn't sustain it and, instead, the docks become the ur-locale of 'Scouse' in his work. Second, and partly because of this failure, the docks become fetishized as the redoubt of 'Scouse': the docks 'will be the last fortress of Scouse when all others are speaking perfect BBC' (Shaw 1960b: 5). The question is, and I have thought about it often, why did Shaw make this argument? The answer has nothing to do with the docks, I think, nor with language in Liverpool, but lies instead in gender politics. For dockers, in Shaw's account but also more generally – it was part of my upbringing – were taken to be the quintessential figure of the Liverpudlian worker: male, working class (and overwhelmingly white). And, as such, they embodied a specific type of cultural identity. The problem is, of course, that this account leaves out all of those women who also worked – in the service industries around the docks but also in the shops, pubs, cafes, schools, factories and so on across the city– and who also spoke Liverpool English. Did they too not create the language of the city? Did they not sustain it? Were they not key to its development in the future? Shaw's work was a crucial contribution to the study of language in Liverpool (and more generally in Britain at a time when most dialectologists were scurrying to rural England to find 'real' dialects). But as in the misogynistic *Learn Yerself Scouse* books, Shaw's achievement is marred by the social prejudices of his day, one of whose effects was to rob women of a voice in the articulation of 'Scouse'.

As it turns out, automation did for the docks as a large employer, and there aren't many Liverpudlians who speak 'perfect BBC' (whatever that means). More importantly, 'Scouse', or Liverpool English, continues to develop. The reason for that is that it was and is a communal language tied to a form of cultural identity, and for that very reason it will continue changing over time. It is stratified and variable, but it is a shared form spoken with modifications across a particular geographic space. It was not and cannot be the preserve of a particular group; as I've learned in my work, it is much too complex and interesting for that.

FOOTY

It was Liverpool against Huddersfield Town, 3pm, Saturday, October 23rd, 1971. Liverpool won 2–0 and the scorers were Tommy Smith, a penalty, on a rebound from the keeper ('Jesus saves ... Smith puts the rebound in', as the graffiti had it), and Alun Evans, 'the first £100,000 teenager'. But the details aren't important. What matters is that I was hooked. From the excitement of the crowd outside the ground, to buying a programme – *The Anfield Review*, 5p – to that first view of that amazingly green pitch as we came up the stairs in the Main Stand, to the noise and the singing on the Kop, to the speed and intensity of the players, to the shared emotions of the supporters – indignation, disappointment, joy and ecstasy by turns. For better or worse, with its ups and downs (like all long-term relationships), footy had me and has me still. Hooked, lined and sunk. That tremor of anticipation and pleasure as you cross Breck Road onto Oakfield Road and go round the little bend for a first sight of the ground ... it's still there, every time. Anfield: grey, angular, drawing us towards it like a huge magnet. A site of passion in both the etymological sense of the term – 'pass', the past participial stem of *patī*, 'to suffer', hence 'suffering' – and its familiar modern meaning – 'strong emotion', 'love'.

The origins of 'Anfield' are unclear. It is probably from 'Hongfield' (1642), 'field on a slope', from the Middle English *hange* + *feld* (which explains Stanley Park). There is, however, an alternative: 'Annefield' ('Gort na hAbhann' – the Riverfield), so named by Robert Graves, an Irish businessman who became Lord Mayor of Liverpool in the nineteenth century, whose family home was 'Annefield' in New Ross, County Wexford. Until the mid nineteenth century, Anfield was still relatively rural, with the occasional villa housing the wealthy. Towards the end of the century, however, Anfield, and neighbouring Kensington, became built up with workers' terraces as a result of urban spread away from the disastrous overcrowding and poor sanitation of the central and dockland areas. Today, despite some development, these remain poor areas, and the contrast with the wealth of the club, and the ridiculous salaries paid to its highest earners, is uncomfortably stark. Of a match day, Anfield is all bustle and hustle, activity and energy; walk around Anfield at other times and it becomes clear how relatively little bustle (in the old slang sense of the term – 'money, ready cash') there is in the area. These days the club makes more of an effort to connect with its local community, but that hasn't always been the case and it's hard to deny that, historically, the club has made a great play of the special relationship between the fans and the team, but it has done very little for the people who live around the stadium. But perhaps that's the reality of it: the significant relationship is between us and the team, and sometimes the manager (Shankly, Paisley, Klopp at least), rather than simply with the club itself, which stands as an enduring business institution. And it is the team rather than individual players that matters. Players, though they depend on us turning up week in week out, can be callous in their indifference; as a kid I spent many a bus journey home from Melwood – Liverpool's training ground – broken-hearted after watching the players speed past in their cars without stopping to sign an autograph. Working-class heroes? That's an ambiguous phrase. Of us they may be (since most footballers are still working class, the exception being the small number of sons of a previous generation of footballers, who went to public schools of course); among us they definitely are not.

But the team have given me some of the great days and nights of my life. Frank Wilson, a centre-forward who played for Blackpool (after being sacked by Spurs for 'insubordination'), died in 1898 of 'maniacal exhaustion caused by football and excitement' – during the close season! I like the sound of this fella, and I know the feeling. It sounds like a description of that ecstasy (Greek ἔκστασις, *ékstasis*, 'insanity, bewilderment') when Liverpool play well, score and win in a big game; there really isn't anything like it. Of course, when I was a kid, right through to my thirties, they won everything and dominated the English game – and Europe to a certain extent. We got used to it, blasé even, until they stopped winning. It wasn't that they weren't successful ... but by the standards they set, it was a long period of disappointment: thirty years was a long time to wait for them to win the league again.

One of my earliest memories is footy-related. I was seated at a first-floor window, looking down on kids celebrating at tables that had been set down the middle of Prophet Street – they'd been borrowed from Coleman's Fireproof Depository, a storage building across Park Road – (I wonder if the owners knew?). I had what we called 'yellow jaundice' (this may seem like an example of pleonasm – more words than you need to express the meaning – since *jaune* is French for 'yellow', but there are three types of jaundice – yellow, black and green), which was probably Hepatitis A. And so, separated above, I had my own jelly and ice cream and watched while the other kids in the street celebrated England's World Cup win in 1966 (or the Jules Rimet Cup World Championship as it was officially known). We had the programme for the World Cup, which featured an advertisement for Lewis's – 'A welcome to all our visitors ... and especially the ladies' – and caused some local indignation by including a map of England with 'distances between staging towns': 'Everton' was marked on the map where Liverpool rightly belonged (Group C matches – Bulgaria, Brazil, Hungary and Portugal – were played at Goodison Park). In fact, the World Cup has a place in the history of Scouse. Frank Shaw had tried to have his glossary of the vernacular published a number of times in the 1950s and early 1960s. The World Cup provided the perfect opportunity as those vast numbers (ahem) of Bulgarians, Brazilians, Hungarians and Portuguese would flood into Liverpool and clearly be in need of a translation tool. And so, just as the official programme for the Jules Rimet Trophy (or at least sections of it) was published in English, French, German and Spanish, *Learn Yerself Scouse* volume 1 appeared in Liverpool bookshops just in time for the World Cup. Key phrases included: 'a game of footee'; 'ere's a good spec' (place to view from); 'anyone gorra proey?' (programme); 'ee wuz wellied' (kicked); 'ee cudden stop a pig in a jigger' (rubbish goalie); 'ee wuz from ere to de Pier ed off' (offside); 'buy a bewk, ref!' (learn the rules) (Shaw 1966a: 48–51).

Needless to say, England wasn't and isn't my team; 1966 was the last time I supported 'the national side' (I was five, I didn't know any better). Though I'd watch footy pretty much anywhere (from the local park to the Nou Camp), Liverpool is my team and Anfield is the place. Of course 'Anfield South' (Wembley), was a home away from home for a long time and my first visit was glorious. Ticketless, we set off on Friday 3rd May, 1974 (me, my brother, my dad and Bobby Midghall) and found a B&B behind Euston Station (we knew it was the place for us – it advertised hot and cold running water and colour TV). As we were leaving for a visit to the West End, we saw Don Revie getting off the train at Euston, whereupon my dad told my brother and I to ask him if he had any 'spares' (tickets). Given that Revie managed our hated rivals Leeds, who'd just beaten us to the league title, it was a slightly optimistic quest (he ignored us). But we did find one ticket in the London Liverpool Supporters Club (in The Three Lords) and one outside the ground just before the match (I still have it – 'The Empire Stadium Wembley, Football Association Challenge Cup Competition Final Tie, Turnstiles C Entrance 12 East Standing Enclosure, £1'). My dad and Bobby Midge saw us into the ground (where my brother and I, aged thirteen and eleven, held on to each other for dear life), before making their way to a church social club near the ground, which was stoned by Arsenal fans just as the match started. The proey (15p) proclaimed in feature articles that it was a 'Great day for Liverpool and the "Kop" choir' and asked whether it would be 'Records all the way for Newcastle today?' They set a record alright – possibly the worst team in a cup final to date; it was 3–0 to Liverpool (with Alec Lindsay's wrongly disallowed first-half goal the best of the lot) and could have been more. A great day indeed.

I spent my teenage years following Liverpool both at home and at opponents' grounds ('aways'), and I owe much of my knowledge of British and European geography to the Reds. But we didn't just watch footy – we played it at any opportunity (and sometimes when there wasn't an opportunity). My most redolent memory is of great ranging games played with a 'casey' (the bladder was encased in leather) on enormous debbies and ollers with as many a side as wanted to play. But there were other forms: intimate games with just a few of us – 'three and in' or 'goalie wet net', and you could even play on your own – 'spot', in which you had to hit the same place on a wall repeatedly, trying to vary pace and spin to change the distance and angle from which you shot. Looking back on the footy games we played, one of the things that strikes me is how regulated they were by moral intuitions of right and wrong, principally with regard to cheating. There were no referees in the big games; one of the local men offered one day but he was refused on the grounds that 'it just causes trouble'. We didn't play offside, but 'goal hanging' was considered unacceptable ('it's not a goal if you just boot it up and he stands next to the goalie'), and though there were fierce arguments, clear fouls were penalized and persistent offenders were told that they were 'not on' (a complex phrase signalling unacceptable behaviour by a communally recognized if non-codified standard). That well-known Irishman the Duke of Wellington supposedly said that 'the battle of Waterloo was won on the playing fields of Eton'; that's as maybe, but it was on the debbies and ollers that the moral sense that carried generations of Liverpool boys through life was formed.

Sometimes I wish I hadn't been hooked that day in 1971; I've probably spent far too much of my life thinking about, talking about, and watching, the aesthetics and athletics of footy – and Liverpool Football Club in particular. And I know the political argument about it being a distraction – the new opium of the masses. I hate the Premiership too, with its ridiculous, blaring self-regard and self-promotion and its nonsensical soul-destroying deals with Murdoch and all. I detest the screaming and shouting of the commentators – 'AND IT'S LIVE' – who sound like they are parodying kids on a school playground (it must be a form of generic training, since they all do it). But, truth be told, my life would have been less rich without footy, of that I have no doubt. Oh, and the word? The *OED* claims 'footy' as an early twentieth-century term for rugby or Australian rules football. In British English, however, it's clear that 'footy' was a Liverpool coinage ('I to the footy game, she to the hell-hole we called home' – O'Mara 1934: 73). But then it's hardly a secret that 'footy' was invented in Liverpool – I mean, ask any Liverpudlian.

GOBSHITE

The art of delivering and taking an insult was, and remains, an important aspect of Liverpudlian social life. Being able to select the most effective means of deprecation mattered, and we learned how to do it from an early age; but being able to deflect an insult was crucial – woe betide you if you showed any sign of being affected by it (you were just asking for worse). Of course, like all forms of language, the power of insults depends on their use in context, including the context of the cultural norms and practices of Liverpool. That may be why some Liverpudlian insults seem harsh to non-Liverpudlians, or indeed why outsiders misunderstand some insults as gentler than they are intended to be (when I used 'soft lad' in Oxford to describe some of my contemporaries, it was often taken to be gently mocking, rather than an expression of complete contempt). Some of the most powerful insults during my childhood were delivered witheringly by women (insults, like slang, may be gendered, but the idea that women use fewer insults than men – or indeed less slang – is dubious to say the least). My nan was a well-versed practitioner of the art of disdain ('nan' is a contraction of 'nanny', though Liverpool also has 'nin', from the Welsh *nain*, 'grandmother'). I very rarely heard her swear, but when a Tory appeared on television her reflex epithets were: 'what do you expect from a pig but a grunt?', and 'more faces than the eye of a fly'. One night, in the Silver Sands – a Somali shebeen (Irish *síbín*, from *séibín*, 'little mug', by extension 'ale, esp. bad ale') on Princes Road – I asked a woman to dance. 'Don't you have to be up for school in the morning?', came the reply. A friend, much amused by this, decided to try his luck. 'I came to dance, lad, not to be laughed at', was the response. Foolhardy, the third of our group swaggered over, to be met with: 'lad, sit down, you smell of sick'. We retired from the fray and I ran to catch the last 86 home; I did, after all, have to be up for school.

All of the common insults are alive and well in Liverpool, particularly those associated with genitalia ('dick', 'cunt', 'prick', 'twat', 'knob' and so on), but some of the older terms, associated with a former way of life, have died out. 'Bloody bucket' was a late nineteenth- century term of abuse, for example, and derived from the bucket used in an abattoir to gather blood for black puddings (hence unclean and disgusting – the bucket, not the black puddings). 'Codshead', retained till relatively recently, is an old insult, first recorded in the sixteenth century ('that jobbernole which men call a codshead' is an eighteenth-century example – surely 'jobbernole'– 'stupid or foolish person' should be revived as a term used to describe prime ministers of recent fame?). 'Moke' died out in the 1960s with the disappearance of horses from the streets (it meant anything equine, from a donkey to a carthorse, and, by metaphorical extension, a fool). 'Old shawl' and 'Mary Ann' were terms for men who did cooking and cleaning. They exemplified a bundle of derogatory patriarchal attitudes in their implicit link between housework, 'effeminacy' and masculinity. The derivation of 'ratbag', 'sconehead', 'sheepshagger' and 'slobbergob' is clear, though all are now dated (if still heard). 'Swiper', meaning a 'heavy drinker, boozer' (it derives from the late eighteenth-century 'swipes', 'beer or dregs'– from the English Northern vernacular 'to swipe', 'to drink hastily and greedily'), has now disappeared. Also obsolete is the most common popular name for a Liverpudlian throughout the nineteenth century: 'Dicky Sam'. The origins of this nickname are not entirely clear, as a correspondent noted in the early nineteenth century: 'we are not sufficiently skilled in Etymological Antiquity to explain to him the derivation of the term DICKY SAM, as applied to the good people of Liverpool' (Anon 1821: 96). But it is probable that this term was originally an insult coined by Lancastrians or Mancunians to refer to Liverpudlians; it appears to be a combination of 'dicky', meaning 'dandy' or 'swell', and 'sam', from 'sammy', 'fool'.

There were, of course, any number of negative terms for women; I say of course because if you look at any historical dictionary you can trace the power relations between the genders through the plethora of vicious terms applied to women (there are few female kinship terms that haven't meant 'prostitute' at some point or other in the history of the English language – 'aunt', 'mother', sister', 'wife' for example). Liverpool words included 'bag', 'boiling piece', 'scrubber' and 'slapper' – a terminology predicated on dehumanization. Others revealed the pressures within women-only groups to conform to determined standards of sexual behaviour – for example, 'she's dirty when she's dollied' (from 'dolled up') and 'she's the talk of the wash-house'. Liverpool English also wasn't short of racial epithets for members of the cosmopolite population produced by its status as a major port (as was; despite recent changes, Liverpool is a lot less diverse now than it was earlier in its history). All of the usual offensive terms were used, together with some that were unique to the city. 'Fluke', for example, referred to a 'Pacific islander' ('"Flukes" we used to call them on account of their flat faces. Hawaiians mostly' O'Mara 1934: 14); it derived from the 'fluke', the common flounder, a flat fish. In Herman Melville's *Redburn* (1849), a novel in which Liverpool featured prominently, Redburn, an American sailor, records that he 'was surprised that a colored man should be treated as he is in this town' (Melville 1849: 256). Judged by

American standards of the day (Redburn is writing of a 'colored' man walking with a white woman), Liverpool may have seemed relatively emancipated. But anyone with any knowledge of the disastrous and bitter history of 'race relations' in the city over the past 200 years could only view Melville's comment with irony. When I was growing up, the polite term (and it was the polite term) for children of mixed heritage, of whom there were a good many, was 'half-caste'; recorded from the late eighteenth century, the derivation is from 'caste', 'race, lineage', from Spanish *casta*, ultimately Latin *castus*, 'pure, unpolluted'. There is much denial, not to say self-deception, in dominant accounts of racism in Liverpool, encapsulated in a comment by Fritz Spiegl (editor of the first *Learn Yerself Scouse* volume) on the term 'smoked Irishman': 'there is nothing abusive about it ... it shows how the Liverpudlian accepts the negro as only another immigrant "Irishman" but with a different skin colour. There is, incidentally, no colour problem in Liverpool' (Shaw 1966a: 12). It is a claim that reveals nothing but the self-blind limits of liberalism.

Some contemporary insults have relatively long historical roots; 'balloon' and 'balloonhead', meaning 'idiot', are related to the seventeenth-century coinage 'balloon', meaning 'empty, hollow' person (borrowed from the Italian *pallone*). 'Soft' was attributed to people from the twelfth century in a number of ways: 'gentle or mild in nature or character'; 'easily influenced or swayed; having little power of resistance to the influence of other persons or things; facile, compliant'. But a seventeenth-century extension to 'more or less foolish, silly, or simple; lacking ordinary intelligence or common-sense; easily imposed upon or deceived' – is the dominant Liverpool sense (as in 'soft lad', 'soft girl' and 'soft arse'). 'Shite', as in 'he is a complete shite', is also an older term. Thomas Urquhart's translation of Rabelais in 1653 has this opening to the inscription of the great gate of Theleme:

Here enter not vile bigots, hypocrites,
Externally devoted Apes, base shites,
Puft up, wry-necked beasts, worse than the Huns,
Or Ostrogots, forerunners of baboons
Curst snakes, dissembled varlots, seeming Sancts,
Slipshod caffards, beggars pretending wants,
Fat chuffcats, smell-feast knockers, doltish gulls,
Out-strouting cluster-fists, contentious bulls,
Fomenters of divisions and debates,
Elsewhere, not here, make sale of your deceits.
(Urquhart 1653: 236)

I've spent time in a few shithouses where that warning might usefully have been posted on the door (not that it would have had much effect). 'Shithouse' in this sense ('dreadful place') is an extension of a seventeenth-century coinage meaning 'toilet' (Old English had *cac-hús*, of which 'shithouse is a literal translation; 'cack' is from the Greek κακός, *kakós*, 'bad, base, evil' – hence 'kakistocracy', 'government by the shittiest'). But 'shithouse' has been further extended in Liverpool to signify a 'mean, despicable person', with the additional nuance of 'cowardice'. 'Blert', meaning 'fool, useless idiot', has a slightly more complicated history. Originally from a northern vernacular term recorded in the early eighteenth century, 'blirt', meant 'an outburst of tears' but developed to mean a useless or cowardly person by the early twentieth century; it strengthened later through a merger with 'blurt', in the sense of 'vagina' (though the link and the etymology are unclear). 'Yard dog', an expression of utter contempt, is a mid twentieth-century extension of the seventeenth-century coinage meaning simply a 'watch dog kept in the yard'. 'No mark', again an utterly condemnatory term, also belongs to the mid twentieth century and may be from the idea of 'making a mark', 'leaving an impression/having an effect' (Melville describes a sailor as 'a person of no mark or influence' Melville 1849: 81).

Other Liverpudlian insults are much more recent. These include 'div' or divvy', again 'idiot, stupid person', from the late twentieth century, derivation unknown, and 'fuckwit', similar provenance, probably by analogy with 'nitwit' or 'dimwit'. 'Knobhead', 'knob-end' and 'bellend' are all late twentieth-century coinages, as is 'dickhead' (although maybe not, since one of the great cant dictionaries of the seventeenth century – *The Canting Academy Or, The Devil's Cabinet* – was published by one Richard Head). 'Scally' is very recent and quite specific, whereas 'wanker' is a general term of abuse whose derivation is unclear; it may derive from the late eighteenth-century Scottish *whang*, 'to beat, whip, flog, thrash'; nineteenth-century English vernacular 'whang', 'throw, drive, pull'; or a late nineteenth-century Americanism 'whang', 'penis'. My favourite Liverpool insult, though, is 'gobshite'. Tom Paulin recalls 'the lovely "gobshite" of the poet Patrick Kavanagh' (Paulin: 1984: 16), and it is a lovely word, full of force and withering contempt. In Liverpool, as well as the general sense of 'idiot', it also carries the extra signification of someone who's both gobby and thick. Its Liverpudlian use is best encapsulated by Alexei Sayle, in a turn of phrase that will resonate with anyone who's spent a lot of time in 'meetings' during the course of their career: 'another few days with those dozy gobshites and I'd have lost me ollies' (Sayle and Stafford 1989: 46). The derivation of this utterly dismissive Liverpudlian insult is unclear. It may be from the Irish English 'gobshell', 'a big spittle direct from the mouth' (from Irish *gob*, 'mouth' and *seile*, 'spit'). On the other hand, of course, it could just be 'gob' and 'shite'.

Thomas Urquhart, by the way, translator of Rabelais (whose work contains many wonderful insults) and describer of Liverpool dives before there were any, coined a fine word in 1652 that we could usefully reintroduce into our contemporary language: 'logopandocie' – a readiness to admit words of all kinds (from the Greek λόγος, *logos*, 'word' and πανδοκεύς, *pandokeús*, 'innkeeper').

HARD

Hardman Street is a focal point in town. It starts at Hope Street, with the Philharmonic pub on one corner and the old School for the Blind on the opposite corner. These are interesting buildings in their own right. The Phil is an ornate palace of Victorian splendour, including marble urinals and sinks in the men's toilets (these are so famous that a warning notice at the door advises 'ladies' to 'ask a member of staff before entering the gentlemen's toilets'). The Blind School, founded by the abolitionist Edward Rushton in 1791, later became the Merseyside Police Headquarters and, later still, the Trade Union Centre. Anyway, Hardman Street, full of restaurants and always chocker, runs down to Georgian Rodney Street (Liverpool's equivalent of Harley Street with its private medical practices). It would be fitting if Hardman Street were named after the Irish-born photographer Edward Chambré Hardman, responsible for some of the most iconic images of Liverpool and surroundings in the twentieth century (including 'The Birth of the Ark Royal' at Cammell Lairds in 1950); his house is now a National Trust property on said Rodney Street. In fact, however, Hardman Street owes its name to the Hardman family, owners of the Allerton Hall estate in the south of the city, whose wealth derived from slavery (the abolitionist William Roscoe later bought the property). Unlike Penny Lane (which pre-dates the slaver after which it is supposedly named – James Penny), Hardman Street really does refer obliquely to the city's bitter history.

We didn't know anything of that when we were growing

up; I thought Hardman Street was named after the hard men of Liverpool (and Little Hardman Street, round the corner, after the little hard men of the place). There were enough of them about – hard men and little hard men – and there are plenty words in Liverpool English related to fighting and violence. 'Hard', in the sense of 'tough and aggressive; prone to violence or disorderly behaviour; belligerent, intimidating', is recorded by the *OED* as a twentieth-century development of one of the oldest senses of the term (dating back to Old English): 'physically strong or robust; capable of great physical endurance and exertion; resilient, hardy; (esp. in early use) bold and vigorous in fighting'. The *OED*'s dating of the more recent sense is slightly odd, however, given that it also cites 'hard man', in the sense of a man '(regarded as) particularly tough, aggressive, and self-assured', from the early nineteenth century. 'Hard man' may be related to the extension of 'hard case', from its earlier senses of difficult circumstances and a complicated or difficult legal case, to its application to persons in the nineteenth century: a criminal, ruthless or aggressive person, or just someone difficult to deal with. This was an American development, probably nautical in origin; Melville uses it in *Redburn*: 'these city lads are sometimes hard cases' (Melville 1849: 29). 'Hard skin' was a Liverpool English version of the same term, though it has been displaced by 'hard knock', as immortalized in the folk-song 'In My Liverpool Home': 'I was born in Liverpool, down by the docks/Me religion was Catholic, occupation hard knock'.

'Bucko' or 'buck' also carried the sense of unruliness; a nineteenth-century extension of the nautical 'bucko mate', its origin was probably originally 'buck', 'the male of several types of animal', though it may have been a truncated version of a direct import from Irish English, ultimately from the Irish *buachaill*, 'boy'. There were also several terms that referred to men (specifically) prepared to resort to violence:

'bad man' (with the nineteenth-century African-American English meaning of 'dangerous, menacing'); 'nutter' (a mid twentieth-century Liverpool coinage, probably from 'nutcase'); 'villain' (from 'villein', a member of the class of serfs in the feudal hierarchy, now often with a strong sense of criminality). There were also adjectives used to refer to these men: 'handy' (accomplished at fighting – 'dextrous with the hands'); 'naughty' (which can be used in a very strong sense – 'utterly reprehensible'); 'word and a blow' (which accurately reflects the precariousness of dealing with some 'hard men': a wrong word is followed by an act of violence).

There are lots of Liverpool English terms related to the act of fighting. They include: 'barney' (from the mid nineteenth-century coinage 'raise a barney', derivation unknown); 'to battle' (a retention of the earliest, narrow sense of the term, from the fourteenth century – 'to fight'); 'coats off' (an adjective meaning 'ready to fight'); 'ding dong' (usually 'to have a ding dong', an extension of the seventeenth-century sense 'to ring like a bell', hence 'monotonous repetition' and then 'to assail with words repeatedly'); 'to give someone down the banks' (to remonstrate or fight, origin unknown); a 'go' (a late nineteenth-century Americanism, from the slightly earlier sense of 'go', 'turn, attempt'); a 'lumber' (related to 'in lumber', 'in trouble'; probably a corruption of the seventeenth-century term 'Lombard', a money-lender or pawnbroker, hence 'in lumber', 'in debt, trouble'); a 'pug' (a fighter, boxer, recorded from the mid nineteenth century; an abbreviation of 'pugilist'); a 'scrap' (a mid nineteenth-century coinage, from the discourse of boxing; possibly from 'scrape'); a 'shindy' (recorded from the early nineteenth century; possibly from the name of a sailors' dance, or the game of 'shinty'); 'to sort out' (recorded from the mid twentieth century, an extension of 'to sort', 'to arrange, put in place'); a 'straightener' (a fight to resolve a dispute, recorded from the late twentieth century; an extension of 'straighten', 'make straight, clear up, put in order'); a 'try' (a challenge, superseded by 'go': 'Immediately, as was the custom, he dared me to "have a try?" (The invitation to fight)' (O'Mara 1934: 77).

There are also plenty of Liverpool English words for the violence involved in fighting. Examples include 'to batter' (to hit repeatedly, first recorded in the fourteenth century); 'to belt' (to strike hard, an extension of the sixteenth-century Scottish *belt*, 'hit with a belt'); 'to bottle' (to hit with a bottle, from the mid nineteenth century); 'to cane' (to beat severely, a recent extension of the seventeenth-century sense of 'hit with a cane'); 'to chin' (a twentieth-century coinage); 'to clew' (now obsolete, but recorded in the mid twentieth century; possibly a variant of a mid nineteenth-century vernacular term 'to claw', 'to hit', from 'claw', 'hand or fist'); 'to clock' (to strike someone in the face, from 'clock', recorded from the early twentieth century for 'face'); 'to crack' (to hit or slap, recorded from the mid fifteenth century, but glossed as 'dialectal and colloquial'; from 'crack', 'to strike with a sharp noise'); 'to crease' (to beat or punish, recorded from the early twentieth century; probably a weakening of a hunting term, 'to crease', 'to stun an animal by a shot in the "crest" or ridge of the neck'); 'to deck' (to knock to the floor, from the nautical 'deck' of a ship); 'to hammer' (to beat severely, a simple mid nineteenth-century extension of 'to hammer', 'to strike with a hammer'); 'to kill' ('to hit, beat, or hurt', is sometimes regarded as an example of Liverpudlian hyperbole, but 'kill', meaning 'strike, hit, beat' is the earliest recorded sense, from the thirteenth century; the meaning, 'put to death', is a fourteenth-century development); 'knock/batter/welly the shite out of' (recorded from the late nineteenth century, unlike 'knock the fuck out of', which is a twentieth-century development); 'to lam'/'to lamp' (recorded from the late sixteenth century; ultimately from the Old English *lęmian*, 'lame'); 'to marmalize' (to beat comprehensively, destroy, punish or chastise; apparently a combination of 'murder', 'paralyse' and 'marmalade' – a

Liverpool coinage popularized by Ken Dodd); 'to nut' (to butt someone, recorded from the mid nineteenth century; an extension from boxing discourse, 'to nut', 'to hit someone on the head'; from the slightly earlier sense of 'nut', 'head'); 'to plant' (to hit very hard, recorded from the early nineteenth century; another borrowing from boxing discourse, but probably originally an extension of 'plant', 'set in the ground'); 'a puc'/'pug' (a blow, strike, recorded from the mid nineteenth century; a borrowing from Irish English, ultimately from the Irish *poc*, 'butt' – by a goat – or a 'stroke of a stick' – as in hurling); a 'smack' (slap, punch, blow, recorded from the late eighteenth century; an extension of 'smack', 'loud noise made by lips'); 'to twat' (to hit very hard, recorded from the late twentieth century; origin unclear in this sense); 'to welly' (to kick, hit; beat up; recorded from the mid twentieth century, an extension of 'welly', 'Wellington boot').

Given the prevailing conditions of patriarchal masculinity (as noted earlier, my school motto was 'Viriliter Age' – 'act like a man'), I was told as a kid that I had to learn 'to look after myself' (a euphemism for being able to fight). And it was true that, in and out of school, a perception that you were at least ready to defend yourself was necessary to fend off the bullies and their friends. I was, I suppose, fortunate in that, aged thirteen or so, I was cajoled into joining the Irish Guards cadets on Windsor Street (the Irish Guards were one of the few British Army regiments barred from serving in Northern Ireland at the time, so it was possible for the Liverpool Irish to sign up). I learnt to box (badly) and shoot (not badly) and, while my skills with a gun have thus far proved redundant, my encounter with pugilism served me well. I haven't hit anyone since I stopped boxing when I was fifteen. Truth be told, I didn't hit many people while I was boxing either – I spent many a three minutes trying to avoid any contact whatsoever – but that was beside the point. At school, the fact that I was in the Guards and boxed was sufficient to deter the more violent of my peers from paying me any attention; it was surely worth the price of the ridiculous haircut I was forced to sport for a couple of years. But it was also at school that I experienced one of the worst types of violent bullying: the vindictive exercise of unaccountable power by teachers over pupils by way of physical abuse. Like many of my contemporaries, I was strapped, poked, punched in the back of the head, hit with a pump, and had my hair pulled; and I was, for the most part, a well-behaved conformist. Though I have much to be enormously grateful for in relation to my education at Sneddies, and a number of teachers whom I happily acknowledge to have been formative and beneficially influential, I find it difficult to forgive the despicable actions of a small minority of teachers (one in particular) who inflicted violence without rhyme or reason. My father was a gentle man, but I didn't tell him until years after I left about the fear and intimidation (often worse than the violence itself) that reigned at school. His reaction told me that I was wise not to have told him.

Partly because I've worked in Northern Ireland on and off for more than forty years, I've spent a long time thinking about violence: its justification (or not), its forms, and its effects. I've seen direct, brutal violence close up, carried out both by the state and paramilitaries. I've also witnessed the long, slow, casually vicious violence of the poverty that the economic order under which we live, and the policies of the state whose function is to maintain that order, inflict on the dispossessed. In that regard, I've met many remarkable men and women to whom the older sense of 'hard' could apply: 'physically strong or robust; capable of great physical endurance and exertion; resilient, hardy'. But I've also met many 'hard' men (in the most recent sense of the term – 'particularly tough, aggressive, and self-assured' describes them perfectly). One of them, an ex-paramilitary who served a long time in jail, put the whole tedious masculine notion of hardness into proper perspective. I have a large archive of photographs from Northern Ireland – murals mostly – so we were talking about murals and commemoration, the war, politics and violence. Someone else in the conversation referred to my interviewee admiringly as 'hard'. 'Hard?', he said, eyeing his mate, 'hard?': 'this is how hard anyone is: someone walks up behind you and smashes the back of your head in with a basie; or they walk up to you and plug you, one to the chest, one to the head to finish you off. End of hard'. 'Or you get some terrible disease', I added, helpfully I thought. There was a long and disconcerting pause, during which I scrambled desperately to remember if any of his family or friends had died from some grim form of cancer. 'Aye', he said softly, 'or that'.

IPPIES AND OZZIES

Returning from a medical appointment at Alder Hey, the children's hospital just down the road from my school, St Edward's, I made my way to my French class and was challenged by the teacher: 'you're late Crowley, where have you been?' As ever the tone was peremptory and admitted of no conclusion other than that I'd been up to some sort of no good. 'I've been to the ozzy, sir', I replied and proceeded to my desk. 'Where are you going? Come back here boy! You've been where?' I was puzzled as I made my way back to the front. 'The ozzy sir, I've been to the ozzy'. 'The what child?' 'The ozzy, sir, where you go to see the doctor; I broke my leg last year'. There was a thundering silence (oxymoronic I know). 'Do you mean the hospital, you stupid boy? The h-ospital?'. I was momentarily stumped, before I realized that he meant what I meant by 'the ozzy'. 'Yes, sir, the hospital'. 'Then say so, boy; put your hand out'. And so I was whacked and learned, annoyingly and painfully, a lesson about linguistic variation, specifically the notion of what linguists (sometimes precisely, often very loosely) call 'style'. In which regard: we read Molière's *Le Bourgeois Gentilhomme* (1670) for A-level. In the play, Monsieur Jourdain is delighted to discover that he has been speaking prose all his life; given that it is a universal characteristic of language use, he might have been similarly pleased to have learned that he spoke with style.

As the example of 'ozzy' shows, there is one stylistic feature that is characteristic of Liverpool English. Linguists don't quite have a name for it; it's often called 'hypocorism', which means the coining of diminutives, or shortened forms, as in the pet-names of children's talk (from the Greek ὑποκορίζομαι, *hupokorízomai*, 'to play the child, talk child language', though Aristotle's *Rhetoric* simply has it as 'to use diminutives'). Indeed, in apparent agreement with this account, in perhaps the first observation on such forms in Liverpool English, John Farrell commented that 'carried into adult usage are many childish abbreviations of doubtless euphony and ease'. Given in two key articles on the language of Liverpool ('Scouse' hadn't yet been invented – see the entry on **Scouse**) in *The Liverpool Echo*, Farrell's examples included 'leccy' (electricity), 'lanny' (landing stage) and 'Scottie Road' (Scotland Road), as in the illustrative sentence: 'he skipped a leccy down Scottie Road to get to the lanny' ('he gets a free ride on the back of an electric tramcar down Scotland Road to reach the landing stage') (Farrell 1950a, 1950b: 4). But the term 'hypocorism' isn't quite right for this feature of Liverpool speech, because in Liverpool 'hypocoristics' are sometimes not diminutives and are in fact longer than, or the same length as, the original terms – as in 'bezzie' for 'best', 'Parkee Lane' for 'Park Lane', and 'spadger' for 'sparrow'. Moreover, they aren't used only by children since they form a central part of adult speech – as in 'Anny Road' for 'Anfield Road', 'binnie' for 'binman', 'ciggies' for 'cigarettes', and 'placcy' for 'plastic'. Another linguist calls the feature the result of a 'prosodically conditioned morphological truncation process' (Honeybone 2007: 122); but that isn't quite accurate either since, apart from the fact that words aren't necessarily truncated (as above), it seems to suggest that the change in the shape of the words is conditioned by pronunciation patterns alone rather than the stylistic 'contexts of situation' in which language is used (as per my 'ozzy' lesson). So what should we call this unusual feature then, which appears as a major characteristic of the form of English used in Liverpool (as well as, incidentally, the Englishes of Australia and New Zealand)? We could call them 'ippies' (short for 'hypocoristics'), but my own technical term for this Liverpudlian changing of the shape of words for various purposes is: 'plazzymorphism' ('plazzy' from 'plastic', in the adjectival senses of 'flexible, able to be moulded' and thus, by extension, 'creative, generative'; 'morph' from the Greek μορφή, *morphé*, 'form, shape').

If John Farrell was the first to remark on plazzymorphs in Liverpool English, other commentators were not far behind. For example, Frank Shaw noted 'the addition of -er to part of a name' as well as '-y or -ey': 'thus we get: Waller (for the Walton Housing Estate), footy, Margy Baths (Margaret Street), Corpy, Neller (for Ned Tarleton), parkey (park-keeper), Delly (Adelphi). Hippy (Hippodrome)' (Shaw 1954: 6). A little later, Richard Whittington-Egan (a feature writer for *The Liverpool Echo*) commented that in Liverpool 'the habit of ellipsis – Butty for a mixture of bread, butter and sugar – is common, and the shortening of words, or apocope, as Conny-onny (condensed milk), Maggy-Ann (margarine)' (Whittington-Egan 1955a: 6). David Isenberg observed that Liverpudlians 'are inclined to cut words short of even add endearing diminutives to them. Hence, I have met with such as "ozzy" (hospital), "rally" (railway), "Pivvy" (the Pavilion Theatre) and "de Pool" (for Liverpool itself)' (Isenberg 1962: 6). And retrospectively (writing of the 1920s and 1930s), Frank Unwin recalled that 'just as the Hippodrome became the "Hippy", the Westminster Theatre the "Wessy" and the Rotunda the "Roundy", so the old Pavilion Theatre in Lodge Lane became known to Liverpool people as the "Pivvy"' (Unwin 1984: 184). Citing the transformation of 'The Theatre Royal Adelphi' to 'the Delly', Liverpudlians, he observed, 'couldn't resist cutting a name down to size' (Unwin 1984: 176).

The use of plazzymorphs then was evidently a well-established feature of Liverpool speech in the 1950s and 1960s. But have they been retained? Here is a select list collated from recent written sources by or about Liverpudians: 'abbey' (abbatoir); 'aereegogs' (airplanes); 'ally' (alsatian dog); 'Aly dock' (Albert dock); 'avvy'/'avo' (afternoon); 'baccy' (tobacco); 'basies' (baseball boots); 'bizzy' (police, probably from 'busybody'); 'blackie' (Black Maria); 'bombdie' (bombed place); 'bommie' (bonfire); 'brekky' (breakfast); 'brickie' (bricklayer); 'bronzy' (bronze tan); 'cannie' (canteen); 'cardie' (cardigan); 'catty' (catapult); 'catty' (Catholic); 'caulie' (cauliflower); 'cem' (cemetery); 'changies' (changing rooms); 'chewy' (chewing gum); 'cockies' (cockroaches); 'coggy' (cocky watchman); 'compo'(compensation); 'conny onny' (condensed milk); 'corpy' (corporation); 'cowie' (cowboy film); 'cozzy' (costume); 'crimbo'/'crizzy' (Christmas); 'cuzzies' (customs officers); 'dee' (detective); 'debby' (débris – wasteland); 'deffo' (definitely); 'digie' (digital radio); 'divvy' (from 'div', 'idiot', origin unknown); 'eppy' (epilectic); 'gozzie' (condom – from 'gossamer'); 'gozzy' (cross-eyed, derivation unclear); 'grotty' (grotesque); 'heapo' (heap); 'jackies' (jack sharps – the stickleback); 'jarmies' (pyjamas); 'nicks' (knickers); 'lecky' (electricity); 'lemo' (lemonade); 'lezzy' (lesbian); 'liblab' (library); 'lippy' (lipstick); 'longees' (long trousers); 'merch' (merchant navy); 'milkie' (milkman); 'mobie' (mobile phone); 'moey' (mouth); 'moggy minor' (Morris minor); 'mingy' (scruffy, from 'minty'); 'muzzy' (moustache); 'natch' (naturally); 'nuddy' (nude); 'offy' (off-licence); 'oggen' (seas, from 'ocean'); 'ollies' (originally from 'alabaster'); 'oller' (hollow); 'ovies' (overtime); 'ozzy white' (Australian white wine); 'para' (paranoid); 'parkie' (park watchman); 'pen'/'penno' (penalty); 'pensh' (pensioner); 'photie' (photo); 'pidge' (pigeon); 'plainees' (plain clothes detectives); the Phil (Philharmonic pub/Hall); 'placcy'/'plazzy' (plastic); 'postie' (postal worker/post office); 'prezzy' (present); 'proddy' (Protestant); 'proey' (programme at the match); 'prozzie' (prostitute); 'queg' (queer); 'quezzie' (question); 'reccy' (reconnaissance); 'rellies' (relatives); 'rozzer' ('police', probably from Robert Peel); 'saddo' (pathetic person); 'saddy' (cruel, from 'sadistic'); 'sarky' (sarcastic); 'sass' (sarsaparilla); 'scrappie' (scrapyard); 'the Shaky' (the Shakespeare pub); 'sharrer' (coach, from 'char à banc'); 'sheepy' (sheepskin coat); 'sidies' (side burns); 'soey' (social security); 'spammie' (love bite, from the 'spam' colours?); 'spec' (place, spot, from 'spectate'); 'spesh' (special); 'sponds' (money, from 'spondulics'); 'steggies' (steroids); 'sterry' (sterilized milk); 'strag' (stray pigeon); 'studie' (student); 'subbie' (sub-contractor); 'sunnies' (sunglasses); 'suzzies' (suspenders); 'tabby' (pensioner, from 'Tabitha'); 'taddies' (tadpoles); 'temazzy' (temazepam); 'tenies' (tenements); 'trabs'/ 'trainees' (trainers); 'trackie' (track-suit); 'tranny' (transistor radio); 'wet neller/nellie' (Nelson cake); 'wool' (woollyback); 'workie' (worker). In addition there are any number of place-name plazzymorphs: 'Eggy' (Aigburth); 'Crocky' (Croxteth); 'Greaty' (Great Homer Street); 'Millie' (Mill Street); 'the Mizzy' (Wavertree Mystery Park); 'Parly' (Upper Parliament Street); 'the Prom' (Otterspool promenade); 'Scotty' (Scotland Road); 'Sevvy' (Sefton Park); 'Skem' (Skelmersdale); 'Tocky' (Toxteth); 'Vauxy' (Vauxhall); 'Wally' (Walton); 'Wayo' (Wavertree).

This is by no means an exhaustive list but, even so, the weight of examples might lead the uninitiated to think that any word can be plazzymorphed. But, as Fritz Spiegl, founder of the Scouse Press (and first flautist with The Phil – the orchestra rather than the pub), warned: 'stranger beware: only some words are suitable for diminution. Try to make up your own and you may stand revealed as an impostor' (Spiegl 2000: 8). Indeed, as all Liverpudlians know, there is nothing more socially awkward than someone who plazzymorphs a word that can't be plazzymorphed. I have never heard anyone call 'Anfield' 'Anny', for example, though calling the Anfield Road end at Liverpool's ground anything other than 'Anny Road', or 'the Anny Road', would be odd. The question is, why do Liverpudlians 'like to "diddy-mize" words'? ('diddy-mize', 'abbreviate', from 'diddy', 'small') (Channon 1970: 102).

Spiegl claims that 'the engaging slovenliness of Scouse speech results in an entirely characteristic use of the shortest possible diminutives' (Shaw 1966a: 10). Apart from the fact that this is inaccurate (as noted above, some 'diminutives' are as long as or longer than the word on which they are based – see 'aereegogs', 'longees', 'nuddy', 'saddo', 'trainees'), there is little to be said about this declaration other than it lays bare the snobbery and prejudice that underpins most forms of linguistic purism. But notwithstanding Spiegl's ridiculous linguistic snobbery, the question remains: why are there so many plazzymorphs in Liverpool speech?

I doubt that the answer to that question lies in stereotypical assumptions about the character of Liverpudlians, nor indeed in the sound patterns of the English language (though these certainly influence how forms are made). I think the answer is to be found in the ways in which language is used within the larger culture of Liverpool. Which is to say that plazzymorphs are used as stylistic feature to signal identity. At a macro level, this relates to the fact that culturally Liverpool is an informal and irreverent sort of place (if there ever was a sense of deference in Liverpool, it died a long time ago – overly formal respect and pretentiousness are cardinal sins). And one way of signalling informality, and thus allegiance to Liverpudlian culture in a broad sense, is by using plazzymorphs. Of course, this can go badly wrong, as my experience with 'ozzy' at Sneddies showed, since there are still stylistic rules about levels of informality in particular contexts; but in general the relationship between plazzymorphs and informality is clear. At a micro level, however, plazzymorphs are used to indicate allegiance to specific forms of identity within Liverpool – either local (knowing the diddy names of places in a particular area), or in relation to the intersections of class, gender and ethnicity (being familiar with the plazzymorphs used by and within particular social groups).

Needless to say, plazzymorphs are not confined to Liverpool and they can be found in many forms of English, though my use of them caused much mirth, sometimes consternation, and occasionally antagonism at Oxford University. But complex and largely unexplored, plazzymorphs are a significant stylistic aspect of Liverpool speech and the process through which they are formed does produce some notable new words. 'Footy' is one example, and 'chippy' another ('chippy' was a Liverpool coinage of the mid twentieth century and came generally to displace 'fish and chip shop').

But probably the best example of a Liverpool English plazzymorph, is 'Scouse' itself, in its primary meaning of a type of stew. 'Scouse' is in fact one of the earliest of our plazzymorphs: it was coined at the end of the eighteenth century as a shortened form of the earlier 'lobscouse', an inferior gruel served on ships. All of which goes to show that stylish Liverpudlians have been ippying and ozzying for a long time.

JIGGER

'Alley' is a medieval borrowing of the French *allée*, 'way, path', ultimately from *aller*, 'to go'. The main *OED* definition of the term is 'a passage between buildings; a narrow street or lane, *esp.* one wide enough only for pedestrians; a back lane. In Britain (esp. *English regional* (*northern*) often denoting a narrow lane running behind rows of houses.' The reference to 'English regional (northern)' is telling, since it draws attention to the geographically specific use of the term. And in fact sociolinguists use different words for 'alley' to measure linguistic variation across the north of England. The variants are numerous and include: 'ginnel', 'snicket', 'gunnel', 'jinnel', 'twitchell', 'jitty', 'gitty', 'ten-foot', 'passage', and 'shut'. In Liverpool the common term that we used, for an alley between working-class terraces in particular was 'jigger', though an earlier synonym was 'jowler' and a later alternative was 'entry'. Other terms included 'back-crack', 'cooey' (apparently unrelated to 'cooee', 'call, signal'), and 'eenog' (probably a 'plazzymorph' for 'entry').

'Jigger' is first recorded in the *English Dialect Dictionary* in 1902 as belonging to Lancashire (Liverpool was in Lancashire at the time; it was later moved to Merseyside). The word was later immortalized by Adrian Henri, in one of his surreal 'Liverpool poems':

> And a Polish gunman young beautiful dark glasses
> combat jacket/staggers down Little St Bride St blood
> dripping moaning clutches/collapses down a back jigger
> coughing/falls in a wilderness of Dazwhite washing.
> (Henri, McGough and Patten 1967: 16)

If the derivation of 'alley' is simple enough, the roots of 'jigger' and 'jowler' are much more obscure. Precisely because of this, these words provoked a spate of indignant and often irate letters to Liverpool newspapers in a correspondence that ranged from the 1930s to the 1950s. As ever in such debates, the lack of knowledge was only matched by the confidence of the etymological speculation. For example, a contributor to the *Liverpool Daily Post* in 1945 claimed that 'jigger' was used primarily in 'the south end of the town' and derived from 'jigger-mast', meaning 'the aft, back or rear' mast on a ship. After all, the writer noted, 'what more applicable term could so briefly express the phrase "back-entry" in such a sea-going community as South Liverpool was in the latter days of the tall ships?' ('Postman' 1945: 6). What indeed? However, an alternative, if somewhat associative, root was provided by another correspondent who claimed that in the Bank of Liverpool (later Martin's Bank and later still Barclays), 'jigger' referred to 'the short vellum markers' inserted in the financial ledgers to mark pages, because 'each marker, or "jigger", represented an "entry"' on a page ('Postman' 1947a: 4). There were also putative accounts of the origin of 'jowler'. One writer claimed that the term belonged to the North End of Liverpool (Everton in particular) and asserted that it differed from 'jigger' in its reference to a 'very narrow type of entry' (rather than a narrow type of entry presumably) ('Postman' 1947b: 6). The origin was given as the verb 'to jowl', first recorded in 1470, meaning 'to dash the head against something' (no further explanation was deemed necessary). A later informant proposed simply that the word 'is derived from the fact that two people can only pass through a "jowler" if they go through "cheek by jowl"' ('jowl' here in the seventeenth-century sense of 'cheek' – hence 'cheek to cheek') (Griffith 1950: 4). In fact, 'jowler' is something of a linguistic puzzle, though 'jigger' is slightly easier to unravel. In his 'Vocabulary of the Flash Language'

(1819), a glossary of underworld terms ('flash') compiled in order to lessen his punishment as a transported criminal, James Vaux gives simply 'JIGGER, a door'. But the clue to its origin lies in Vaux's observation that 'to speak *good flash* is to be well versed in cant terms' (Vaux 1819: 183). Cant was the secret language of the underclass and 'jigger' is first recorded in Thomas Harman's *A Caveat for Commen Cursetors Vulgarley called Vagabones* published in 1567 (the title might be rendered into modern English as 'A warning against common travellers popularly called vagabonds'). Interestingly, this glossary of cant was published almost forty years before the first dictionary of English proper (Robert Cawdrey's *Table Alphabeticall* appeared in 1604). In his *Caveat*, Harman records 'a gyger, a dore' (a jigger, a door) with an illustrative quote: 'Towre ye yander is the kene dup the gygger, and maund that is beneshyp' ('See you, yonder is the house, open the doore and aske for the best') (Harman 1567: n.p.). One source gives an even older root for 'gyger'. Charles Ribton Turner's *History of Vagrants and Vagrancy and Beggars and Begging* (1887) suggests that the origin of the term lies with the Welsh *gwddor* – pronounced 'gigger' – which he gives as 'gate' (though older Welsh dictionaries say 'wooden bridge'). But if the root is old cant, and/or Welsh, what is the route by which 'jigger' became the Liverpool word for an alleyway? Sadly, we don't know; words move in mysterious ways, their wonders to perform.

As noted above, our other word for a 'jigger' was an 'entry'. In its original use, 'entry' meant an approach to, or passage leading to, a building – as in Chaucer's *Knight's Tale* (c1385): 'The temple of Mars ... of which the entree/ Was long and streit, and gastly for to see' (Chaucer 1988: 52). But in this sense, it meant the front of a building. In Liverpudlian usage, however, the 'entry' was the alley that ran behind and between rows of houses. Despite that, the term retained its meaning of 'entrance' for one very good reason: in working-class

Liverpool, the main access to a house was often the back rather than the front. Like the usually unused front parlour (from the French *parler*, 'to talk', hence 'conversation room'), the front door was for special visitors and special occasions. It was parlous (a variant of 'perilous') to use it otherwise. Woe betide the kid who knocked on my nan's front door (with its brassoed handles and donkeystoned step) for no good reason. Once, returning from school to my nan's house, freezing cold on a bitter winter's day, I banged on the front door and waited in vain; when I eventually 'went round the back' to the entry and through the back yard, I found my nan cooking in the kitchen. 'Why didn't you open the door?', I asked. 'I wasn't expecting anybody', came the sharp reply.

'Jiggers' were important, if hazardous, play areas. You pelted down them in games of 'Kick the Can', or 'Rallio', dodging dog-shit, vermin of various sorts, strange yellowy-white crumpled up balloons (we were too innocent to know) and, in Prophet Street at least, bins hanging off the wall full of pink-grey fire ash from the fires that heated (or not) the terraced houses on either side. By day they were hunting grounds where we found the most enormous green and orange slugs; they were, I'm ashamed to say, blown up with bangers or other fireworks in the run up to Bommie night (two or three piled together could cover half a backyard wall). By night, however, jiggers were different places altogether – frequented by that very dangerous breed, the courting (not to say sexually engaged) couple whose wrath, once provoked, knew no bounds (especially the male of the species). In some jiggers, where the width was only a few feet, you could leap from back wall to back wall and, if you timed it right, you could catch someone in an outside toilet. Creeping on to the slabbed roof of such a *cac-hús* (the accurate term), and then stamping your feet as loudly as possible, led to a reaction to be compared only with that of the aforementioned coitors interrupted. One occupant staggered out, trousers hastily pulled up, shouting, appropriately, 'shithouses'. All that stopped when we moved to Springwood, a 1930s council estate on the Garston/Allerton borderline. There were no jiggers there, though you could hedge-hop (crash through the hedges) between front gardens; from privies to privets – a step up in the world, you might say.

The jigger rats were the key to that move, which was geographic (it was five miles towards the southern end of the city) and social (Springwood was a very different community to the Dingle, and the houses had indoor bathrooms and toilets). I later discovered that we'd followed South Liverpool FC (The South), which began in Dingle Lane and ended up in Holly Park, also on the Garston/Allerton boundary border, next to 'the Bridge' that carried the railway line south and traversed Mather Avenue, as Garston's own fine poet Peter Robinson describes it:

> Copper-oxide-coloured ledge
> Slung between two brick supports,
> the bridge
> marks the line's trajectory,
> bisected by the avenue.
> (Robinson 1996: 145–6)

Holly Park hosted some notable games before it closed in 1990. It staged the first floodlit football game on Merseyside in 1949, and in 1967 the Real Madrid star Ferenc Puskás played in a charity match against a team led by the Liverpool legend Billy Liddell. I was there, and afterwards I queued up for Billy's autograph and ignored Puskás (World Cup finalist, three times winner of the European Cup, ten times winner of the Spanish league, and top goalscorer of the twentieth century). Parochialism runs deep. Next to Holly Park was a good spec to watch Liverpool embark on one of their victorious tours of the city celebrating yet another triumphant season after they got off the train Allerton Station (this was before footballers flew the short distances from one British city to another). A couple of days after one such return, I saw Jimmy Case coming out of one of the local shops (his mum lived on the estate). Case had completed the journey that we all wanted to make: he played for South Liverpool before winning the league (four times) and the European Cup (three times) with Liverpool. 'Alright kids', he said as he passed; it took me days to recover.

Anyway, the rats. The back yard and jigger behind our house at 33 Prophet Street (seven of us lived in a three-roomed flat above a disused shop) was full of rats – you had to stamp your feet to make them scatter when you opened the back door to go to the toilet. Young kids couldn't be left outside the door in a pram for fear they'd be bitten. My parents had applied for a move, but the perennial housing crisis in Liverpool (which dated back to the nineteenth century) meant that there was little chance, even though we were on 'the list' and had the points to qualify. The housing inspector came on a regular basis – to inspect what I'm not quite sure – and on one occasion, the last as it turned out, he returned to his car to find three dead rats in a plastic bag on his front seat with a note: 'We have to live with them – see how you like it'. The culprits were never identified but I reveal them now: my dad, his brother Teddy, and his brother-in-law Billy Midghall. We moved not long afterwards.

KOP

The Second Boer War (or the Second War of Independence as the Boers called it) was an important colonial dispute between British Imperial forces and the Boers of the South African Republic, known then as the Transvaal, and the Orange Free State. The war was ugly and featured the implementation by the British of concentration camps by Lord Kitchener – 'Your country needs you to imprison women and children' – and a brutal 'scorched earth' policy. Largely motivated by gold, diamonds and the interests of the British Empire against those of the descendants of Dutch settlers, the war featured the native black population in only limited, though still substantial, roles. In January 1900 a battle took place near Ladysmith, near Natal, for a scrubby, relatively small, but strategically significant hill. Named Slag bij Spionkop in Dutch (Dutch was the written language of the Boers at the time), and Slagg van Spioenkop in Afrikaans, the Battle of Spion Kop saw a Boer victory against superior numbers, and the capture of the 'spy hill' (Dutch *spion*, 'spy' and *kop*, 'hill, outcrop'), with considerable loss of life on both sides. As well as Winston Churchill and Mahatma Ghandi, British forces included a large number of Liverpool soldiers in the Eleventh Brigade (consisting of the Second King's Royal Lancaster Regiment, the Second Lancashire Fusiliers, and the First South Lancashire Regiment), among whom there were many casualties.

When Liverpool started rebuilding Anfield in 1906 (founded in 1892, they'd just won their second league title), they decided on a new terrace at the Walton Breck Road end of the ground. Brick and cinder, open roofed until 1928, and with a capacity of 26,000, it became the largest covered terrace in the league. There were 100 steps at the back and, at the junction with Kemlyn Road, stood a flagpole (it was the mast of the Great Eastern – erected in 1892 while Everton were still the tenants at Anfield). 'The flag', either the Liver Bird or the league championship pennant, was almost as famous a meeting place for older Liverpool supporters as 'Dicky Lewis' was for Liverpudlians in general. 'Dicky Lewis', for the incognoscenti, is the Liverpool nickname for Jacob Epstein's 'Liverpool Resurgent' (1956), a sculpture of a man standing on the prow of a ship looking forward (the work symbolizes Liverpool's rebuilding after the devastation of the Second World War). 'Lewis' registers the fact that the statue is set on the famous department store, 'Lewis's'; 'Dicky' alludes to the fact that the male figure is prominently naked.

The new terrace was christened the 'Spion Kop' when it was first built, in recognition of the sacrifice of the Liverpool soldiers at the Slag bij Spionkop (and perhaps its resemblance to that scrubby hill in South Africa). As the *Liverpool Echo* presciently reported: 'this huge wall of earth has been termed "Spion Kop", and no doubt this apt name will always be used in future in referring to this spot' ('Spion Kop' 1906: 3). My own introduction to the Kop, like that of most boys, was indirect, in that we went to 'the Boys' Pen', a fenced-in enclosure at the top right of the terrace. I've often wondered whether 'the Pen' was used in the sense of 'a fold for smaller animals', or the place where you did your penance (the 'penitentiary'). In any case, it wasn't the best place to watch the match. It was often frightening, with a good number of young bullies ('lend us your scarf lad') and precocious adolescents desperate to escape into the Kop. Despite the presence of a couple of policemen – there were no cops on the Kop itself – there were always some escapees who managed to make it over the barbed wire to freedom. Graduating to the Kop was part of the rite of passage for a young Liverpool supporter. 'Koppite' was recorded as early as 1914; it was an identity I eagerly embraced – not least because I couldn't wait to get away from the Pen.

In the 1970s, all games started at 3pm on Saturday and 7.30pm on Tuesday or Wednesday without exception (well, apart from the games that were played during the blackout period in 1974 – another period of Tory crisis). The Kop opened its doors on Saturdays at 1pm, fully two hours before the match started, and I'd be there with some mates waiting. Often I would have been to the ice-rink on Prescot Road; I wasn't very good at ice-skating, but it was a good place to bump into girls (literally) and to fall on your arse in front of them (literally and metaphorically). This meant that the mile and a half walk to Anfield was conducted in what can only be described as cold, slushy trousers. I longed for the Kop to fill; I could begin to thaw out. Once the game had started of course – after the pre-match preliminaries, which consisted of running through the Kop's extensive repertoire and culminated in 'You'll Never Walk Alone' as the teams came out – things warmed up considerably. Getting there early to get your spec was an important part of the ritual, though after kick-off the crowd cascaded down and poured back, like a film of a waterfall running and reversing. You had to be able to manage your cadences on the Kop – in terms of music and movement – and people rarely ended up exactly where they thought they should be. Looking back on it now, of course, even though effectively self-regulated, it was potentially dangerous; when Liverpool scored, we laughed as we fell forwards on top of people and dragged each other up. Hillsborough put an end to all that, and much else besides.

At a game recently, someone in front of us said in an argument with his mate: 'I've been coming here for fifteen years, pal'. At which point, someone in our row leant forward and said, in the sort of stage whisper you could have heard in the Anny Road: 'don't be saying that lad, people will think you're a friggin blow-in'. I've been watching from the Kop for the best part of fifty years, and I've seen some amazing games and had the most fantastic times. I've witnessed Liverpool win championships, beat the best teams in Europe, and parade trophies the ground in the full confidence that they'd be doing it again next year. I've seen the Reds dominate teams routinely, make the most incredible come-backs, and even, on occasion, get beaten (Red Star Belgrade beat Liverpool 2–1 in the European Cup in 1973 – they were so good it was like looking into the future). They've thrilled me and they've broken my heart. But there is one evening on the Kop that I can't forget, no matter what. It was May 26th, 1989, the last game of the season; Arsenal came to Anfield needing to win by two or more to deny Liverpool the title and the (League and FA Cup) Double. They scored their second with effectively the last kick of the game. It should have been heart-breaking, and any other season it would have been, but it wasn't any other season; the Kop stayed on to applaud Arsenal as they lifted the title.

It wasn't any other season because a month or so earlier Hillsborough had happened. I find it hard to write about Hillsborough. Like any tragedy, there is something ineffable about it. If you want the brutal facts, read the final edition of Phil Scraton's *Hillsborough The Truth*; I don't cry much – a victim of the norms of my masculinist upbringing – but I wept my way through that book. Suffice to say that Hillsborough was not caused by fans who were late, or drunk, or ticketless; it was caused by the police, and they and their vile friends in the right-wing media (led by *The Sun* newspaper) lied about it and have been lying about it ever since. The Liverpool fans who died that day – 'the 96'– were 'unlawfully killed', in the words of the 2016 coroner's report, and no one has ever been held legally accountable. Hard to believe, still hard to take.

The effects of Hillsborough on Liverpool and Liverpudlians are difficult to estimate. My own view is that although Liverpool is and has been a solid Labour town for a long time, Hillsborough contributed significantly to the radicalization of the city. And we have the families and the campaigners to thank for that; their determination and perseverance over almost thirty years brought about a result that many considered impossible: they fought with radical hope in their hearts, and they forced the truth out of the state. It stands as a remarkable achievement – as does the fact that there is a total eclipse of *The Sun* in Liverpool. Whenever I go to Anfield now, like many others I pay homage before the match at the Hillsborough shrine. I look at the names and I think of the familes, and the title of the final report into the disaster in 2017 always, always, comes to my mind: *The Patronising Disposition of Unaccountable Power.*

That Arsenal game wasn't the first that I attended after Hillsborough. In fact I went to the first game that Liverpool played – against Everton at Goodison, as it happened, a terrible 0–0 draw. I felt guilty about going that night, but I also felt that, if I didn't go, I might never go again. I sat next to two Evertonians, a man and a woman. I've come across some good swearers (it's a social skill), but I've never met anyone as capable of vicious, pertinent and sustained swearing as that woman. She cursed Liverpool players from just after kick-off till the end of the game. Her husband sobbed for ninety minutes and I held his hand; his brother (you can be brothers and support different teams in Liverpool) had been crushed at Hillsborough but survived. Everton did Liverpool proud that night. Liverpool fans didn't walk alone then, and they haven't since. In 2012, when the first inquests were set aside, again at Goodison, a girl in an Everton kit and a boy in a Liverpool kit, wearing 9 and 6 on their shirts, walked hand in hand across the pitch before the game to the tune of 'He Ain't Heavy, He's My Brother' (and sister, daughter, mum, grandma, aunty, niece, son, dad, grandad, uncle, nephew, and all). You can call that sentimentality if you like; solidarity would be another word. Fierce rivals? For sure. But some things are transcendent and, notwithstanding the ignorant behaviour of some of Everton's followers at recent derby games, Liverpool fans would do well to remember the sustained support of the vast majority of Evertonians when they throw 'the bitters' taunt.

At the end of the Arsenal game, I turned to a friend who happened to be a Gooner (we'd got him a ticket) and said 'well done, congratulations'. Given that we were standing on the Kop at the time his look of terror might have been merited (there weren't many Arsenal fans on the Kop that night). Except, of course, it wasn't. It wasn't that we didn't care; we cared alright. It wasn't that we weren't disappointed; we were gutted. But we knew, properly, that there were far more important things than league titles to be concerned about. Bill Shankly, one of our greatest managers, once joked: 'some people believe football is a matter of life and death … it's much, much more important than that'. It was amusing when he said it, partly because we knew that it wasn't true. But after Hillsborough, it stopped being funny. Jurgen Klopp, our current manager – honest, funny, passionate, and, as we say, 'sorted' – told it like it is: 'football is the most important of the least important things'.

Though still loud (very loud) raucous, rude, funny, passionate, partisan and generous, the Kop is different nowadays. Its name has changed for one thing – the colonial link has been hidden by the dropping of 'Spion'. More importantly, it's been rebuilt and, like most major football stadia, it's relatively comfortable; you can watch telly beforehand, you can buy something to eat, booze and place a bet if you want to, and use the clean toilet facilities. It's also completely and utterly safe. And that's another enduring legacy for which we can thank the Hillsborough families.

LIVERPOOL

It's a strange thing, but I can see the name 'Liverpool' in a page of text without looking for it; it seems to leap out at me. I don't know why it is – perhaps it is a common experience, I'm not sure. But where does the name of the city come from? Do place-names have etymologies? It turns out that they do, although they are often complex and sometimes a-swirl in a pool of supposition and myth. So what about 'Liverpool'?

In 1207, exercising his royal prerogative, King John swapped Lea, near Preston, for Liverpool, in order to use it as a base for his Irish campaigns (the first link in what was to become the deep historical connection between Liverpool and Ireland). In the *Carta Regis Johannis* (Liverpool's Charter), John declared: 'Sciatis quod concessimus omnibus fidelibus nostris qui burgagia apud Liuerpul ceperint, quod habeant omnes libertates et liberas consuetudines in villa de Liuerpul quas aliquis liber Burgus super mare habet in terra nostra' ('Know ye that we have granted to all our faithful people who may have taken burgages at Liverpul that they may have all liberties and free customs in the town of Liverpul which any free borough on the sea hath in our land') (Picton 1875: 10). In 1229 a second charter was granted by Henry III to 'villâ nostrâ de Leverepul' ('our town of Liverpool') (Brooke 1853: 26). Keen readers will notice the difference between 'Liverpul' and 'Leverepul' and the orthographical variation of the name was not missed by Liverpool's first historian William Enfield: 'concerning the name in question, we find it spelt in ancient records and books in a great variety of ways.

In Cambden's Britannia it is called *Litherpoole*; in Leland's Itinerary, *Lyrpole*, alias *Lyverpoole*; in Morery's Dictionary, *Lerpoole*, or *Leerpool*; in some ancient writings, *Livrepol*, *Lyverpol*, and *Leverpole*' (Enfield 1773: 2).

Such differences seem odd to us, but earlier in the history of the language, variable spelling of the same linguistic form was common. Shakespeare signed his own name in three different ways – Shaksper, Shakspere, and Shakspeare – while there were any number of variants used by others within his lifetime, including Shakespeare, Shakespear, Shakspeare, Shackspeare, Shakspere, Shackespeare, Shackspere, Shackespere, Shaxspere, Shexpere, Shaxpere, Shagspere, Shaksper, Shaxpeare, Shaxper, and Shake-speare. Our sense of the strangeness of such differences ('yes, but surely only one of these was the right spelling?') is a matter of history: we live this side of the stabilization of English spelling, which occurred, more or less, in the eighteenth century. If there is no fixed, codified, and recognized form, then there is no incorrect form, there is just variation. In the case of Liverpool, the current spelling appeared relatively late; Enfield's account of the town was entitled *An Essay Towards the History of Leverpool* (1773).

James Picton, architect and major public figure in nineteenth-century Liverpool (hence the Picton Reading Room – modelled on the old British Library Reading Room – in the Central Library), commented on the name of the city: 'many conjectures and etymologies have been hazarded, but none has hitherto been found which meets with general acceptation' (Picton 1875: 16–17). A century and a half later, that more or less remains true. The first etymologist to try his luck was William Camden in *Britannia* (1590): 'ubi Litherpoole floret, Saxonicè Lyferpole, vulgò Lirpoole, a diffusa paludis in modum aqua, vt opinio est, nominatus' ('where Litherpoole flourishes, in Saxon Lyferpole, in common use Lirpoole, so named, opinion has it, for the way the water spreads as a pool')

(Camden 1590: 614). A century or so later, William Baxter's *Glossarium Antiquitatum Britannicarum* (1719) pronounced that 'hodiernum verò loco nomen Lither-pool est, sive *Pigra palus*' ('the present name in truth is taken from the location – Lither-pool or *sluggish swamp*') (Baxter 1719: 213). Thomas Carlyle used this account in his speculative vision of twelfth-century Liverpool in *Past and Present* (1843): 'The Creek of the Mersey gurgles, twice in the four-and twenty hours, with eddying brine, clangorous with seafowl; and is a Lither-Pool, a lazy or sullen Pool, no monstrous pitchy City, and Seahaven of the world! The Centuries are big; and the birth-hour is coming, not yet come' (Carlyle 1918: 79).

The difficulty in understanding the name 'Liverpool' lies with the first part of the word, as Enfield observed:

> Some suppose that the former part of the name is derived from a bird which used to be found in this place, and was called the *Liver*; but this bird does not appear to have had any existence except in fabulous tradition and in the herald's office. Others imagine that it might have been taken from a seaweed, now known by the name of Liver in the West of England, or from a species of the *Hepatica*, vulgarly called Liverwort, often found on the sea coast: and others who favour the orthography above established, suppose that it might be derived from the *Lever* family, which is of ancient date in this county ... With respect to the latter part of the name, it seems generally agreed that it took its rise from a body of water formerly spread there like a pool. (Enfield 1773: 3)

'Pool' does indeed seem clear enough, but to what does 'Liver' refer? It was the subject of endless speculation. Troughton's *History of Liverpool* (1810) identified the 'lever' bird as a common heraldic device among the Lancashire gentry and noted its history: 'denominated by Conradus Gessner, in Latin, Platea, which he conceives to be the Water Pelican, or Shoveller (Anglice); but in the Dutch it is called Lepler, or Lepelar, or Leefler; in the German, Lefler, or Lever; and it is supposed to be the Spoonbill of Mr Ray, and the Pelican of Onocrotalus' (Troughton 1810: 17). Troughton's own take was that 'if such a bird really exists in nature', it is 'no other than the blue duck, which sometimes frequents our coast, and is also found in the river Ribble, known at present by the name of the *Blue Shoveller* (the *Anas Clypeata of Linnaeus*)' (Troughton 1810: 17). A little later, the important historian of Lancashire, Edward Baines, dismissed the ornithological account by referring to the image of a bird presented on the town's historic seal:

> The head of this bird seems to be the head of a dove; but the eagle of Tarbock has been mistaken for a dove, and recently for a green parrot. The eagle of the Stanley crest has the neck of a stork or goose. In deriving the name of the town from this imaginary bird, which was unknown long after the town had a common seal, we have a remarkable instance of putting the cart before the horse. (Baines 1836: 58)

Or the bird before the name. Likewise shying away from calling the mighty Liver Bird a duck, Troughton favoured another explanation based on Camden's 'Litherpool': 'The word *lither* signifies *lower*, so that Lither-pool means simply the *lower pool*. Hence the name of the village of Litherland, or lower land; and of a passage, yet called Litherland Alley, in the neighborhood of Pool-lane, corroborates our assertion, that the foregoing is the original derivation of the name of the town' (Troughton 1810: 20). No sooner was this account published, than it was contradicted by W.R. Whatton, who argued that the first part of the name derived from the Anglo-Saxon adjective *lið, liða, liðe* (soft or gentle, calm, slow or mild), hence, by 'joining the adjective Liðe with the Saxon substantive word pol, or more properly pul, lacus, we have Liðepul, a still or quiet lake'. 'Nothing', he added, 'can be more beautiful or expressive than this simple term when applied to the harbour of Liverpool as it must have appeared during the Saxon æra, with its fenny banks, and quiet waters, as yet undisturbed by the busy hum of men' (Whatton 1817: 508). Well quite.

The historical study of language made great progress during the nineteenth century and one of its most important figures was the etymologist and dialectologist W.W. Skeat. Focussing on that problematic first element, Skeat rejected earlier explanations of the first element in 'Liverpool' in favour of the Anglo-Saxon word *læfer* (pronounced 'lavver'), given in Oswald Cockayne's *Leechdoms, Wortcunning, and Starcraft of Early England* (1886) as 'gladiolus' or 'bull-rush', and the related terms 'lĕver' or 'liver', defined in Britten and Holland's *English Plant-Names* (1866) as 'any sword-bladed plant' such as the iris, bur-reed or gladiolus. Skeat concluded: 'putting all this together, we see that the name liver was certainly applied to some kinds of the iris and the bulrush which grew in pools. When it appears that *liver*-pool, originally, meant more nor less than "a pool in which livers grew," meaning by liver some kind of water-flag or bulrush. And this is all!' (Skeat 1896: 174).

Sadly, it wasn't all. Henry Harrison, author of *The Place-Names of the Liverpool District* (1898), rejected Skeat's conclusion, along with the idea that 'Liverpool' was a derivation from a 'hypothetical Celtic' root: '*Llyrpwll* (Welsh *llyr*, "brink," "shore," "sea")' and 'Cymric *pwll*' (Harrison 1898: 28–9). Instead, he adopted a suggestion made by H.A. Strong, Professor of Latin at Liverpool University, that 'Liverpool' was indeed derived from 'Litherpool', and that this was 'like so many others in its vicinity, a Norse name, meaning, "pool of the slope or brow," O[ld] N[orse] *hliþ* = a slope; cf. Litherland, a suburb of Liverpool, near Crosby, and a numerous list of place-names similarly formed in Vigfusson's "Dictionary". The Norse word is connected with the Lat[in] *clivus*' (Strong 1896: 233). Harrison continued:

In Old Norse we find *hlíthar-brún*, 'the edge of a slope,' *hlíthar-fótr*, 'the foot of the slope,' so that there would not be too much difficulty about *hlíthar-land*, 'the land of the slope' or 'the slope land,' and *hlíthar-pollr*, 'the pool of the slope'... It is scarcely necessary to point out that the Norse element in the vicinity of Liverpool was very strong; and the appropriation of creeks and sea-pools, and of land adjacent to the coast, was a well-known characteristic of the ancient Norwegians and Danes. (Harrison 1898: 30)

There is certainly linguistic evidence of Viking settlement around the Mersey (in place-names such as Skelmersdale, Aigburth, Formby, Crosby, Toxteth and Croxteth), but in Wyld and Hirst's *The Place Names of Lancashire* (1911), 'Liver' was explained alternatively as a derivation of the Old English personal name *Léōfhere*, and so 'Liverpool' meant 'Léōfhere's pool' (as in 'Otterspool', derived from 'the pool of Ohthere', rather than the commonly supposed pool of the otters) (Wyld and Hirst 1911: 179–80). But Eilart Ekwall (1922) denounced that derivation, arguing instead that 'Liver- is to be compared with O[ld] E[nglish] *lifrig* (in *lifrig blod*), M[iddle] E[nglish] *livered*, "coagulated, clotted."' Citing the *OED*, he noted the use of 'liver-sea' (1600) 'an imaginary sea in which the water is "livered" or "thick," and concluded that '*Liverpul* may mean "the pool with the thick water"'. Which sounds a lot like what Baxter said in 1719.

If, like me, you're sorry you started on all this and just want to know the origin of the word 'Liverpool', I have to disappoint you: we don't know. And the Liver Bird? The *OED* says this:

A 14th-cent. seal from Liverpool shows a bird apparently intended to represent an eagle (symbolizing St. John the Evangelist). Legend has it that poor draughtsmanship led to the bird being variously identified as (amongst others) a spoonbill, a glossy ibis, and a pelican. Since the late 18th cent. the bird represented on modern grants of arms, etc., has been identified with the cormorant.

In other words, the Liver Bird began as a badly drawn eagle, which morphed later into a bird often known as the common shag. And there we'll leave it but for one thing. No offence to the good people of Lea, but I think King John got the better of that deal in 1207.

MERSEY

Physical geographers tell us that the River Mersey is about seventy miles long, springing from the confluence of the Goyt and the Tame in Stockport and flowing to Liverpool Bay where it meets the Irish Sea. Its tributaries include the Irwell and the Weaver and it becomes tidal at Warrington; it is three miles at its estuarial wide point. Cultural geographers, on the other hand, might note that the name of the river derives from the Old English *mǣre* (genitive *-s*) 'boundary' + *ēa* – 'river' – (the boundary in question being that between the old kingdoms of Northumbria and Mercia). Historically, the Mersey clearly marked a boundary to cross. Today there are six ways to traverse the river: ferry (with 'Ferry Across the Mersey' rather self-referentially blaring out), rail, two road tunnels and two bridges. Boat is the oldest way of crossing; Benedictine monks began a ferry service in the twelfth century, no doubt singing 'pontonis trans Belisama' (Ptolemy's Latin name for the Mersey).

The Mersey was ever-present in my childhood and occasionally it haunts my dreams still. Northumberland Street – yards from where I was born – ran west down to 'the river' (as we called it), and the other places in which I grew up – Lascelles Road on the Springwood estate in Allerton and Stormont Road in Garston (my nan's house) – were both within fog-horn distance of the Mersey. If you looked down Northumberland Street you saw Cammell Laird's on the other side, and a procession of tankers making their way to Port Sunlight oil terminal. But if you walked round the corner and up to the top of Park Road and looked south, west and north respectively, you could see the river curving and silvering away towards Widnes and Runcorn, or lying grey and flat beneath the brown banks of Birkenhead and the distant North Welsh mountains, or pulling hazily past the Liver Buildings to the Irish sea beyond. From Lascelles Road you could hear the river at night, but to see it you had to walk a quarter of a mile to Clark's Gardens, the estate on which stood William Roscoe's Palladian Allerton Hall. From the small incline behind the pillbox at the corner of Woolton Road (installed to defend against Nazi invaders, we were told) you could look over Allerton cemetery to the river and Moel Famau in North Wales.

Always shining or grey at a distance, full of murky browns close up, the river was a mystical and mythical place. Both of my grandfathers worked on it as dockers, through all the viciousness of the casual labour scheme (the 'gig economy' before the term was invented – a model of the true relations between capital and labour), as did other male relatives, though many local men had also spent part of their working lives as sailors in the Merchant or Royal Navy. Most of the naval trade had gone by the time of my childhood, and the scale of the docks had been reduced greatly, but the river and its history were still treated with what seemed like reverence. In my maternal grandmother's house I was told of the dinner-time visits of Jack Jones – docker, Spanish Civil War veteran and later leader of the Transport and General Workers' Union (and as such described and vilified by the *Daily Mail* as 'the most powerful man in Britain' during the mid 1970s); his sister, Winnie, was a friend and neighbour of my nan. Jones ascribed his conversion to socialism to his reading of Robert Tressell's *The Ragged-Trousered Philanthropists*; it took me a while to get round to that – my childhood reading (and avid rereading) was largely confined to *Newnes' Pictorial Knowledge* (published in the late 1920s in seven volumes).

One of the editors of that work was Enid Blyton; Noddy, however, it wasn't. The texts, beautifully illustrated with detailed images and photographs, might better have been described as an encyclopaedia of imperial knowledge and it included 'A children's dictionary – unusual and difficult words simply explained'. I later found out that dictionaries were originally collections of 'glosses' (from Latin *glossa*, 'a hard word in need of explanation') – hence 'glossaries'. The first English to English dictionary (really an extended glossary) was Cawdrey's *Table Alphabaeticall* (1604); it was written for 'Ladies, gentlewomen, or any other unskilfull persons' – an insight into the relations between literacy, gender and class at the time. 'Unskilful person' covered me; if I didn't know the meaning of a word, my dad told me to 'look it up' (I can hear his voice saying it now). Perhaps that childish dictionary was where my fascination with language began.

We called the *Newnes* our 'encyclopaedia', which is an interesting word, not least in the fact that it is a pseudo-Greek invention or misreading by Latin writers (based on the Greek ἐγκύκλιος παιδεία, *enkúklios paideía*, 'the circle of arts and sciences' considered to be the core of a liberal education). Volume three of the encyclopaedia contained extensive articles on such gems as 'The Temple of the Tooth', 'Mother Ganges', 'Kraals of the Kaffirs', and 'An Australian Sheep Station', amongs its telling of 'The Story of the World and its Peoples. The Empire on which The Sun Never Sets'. It would be unfair, though, simply to dismiss it as imperial fodder since its more than 3,000 pages covered a wealth of historical, literary, cultural and scientific knowledge that kept me enthralled (including a beautifully detailed and layered dissection of a 'green water-frog' – *Rana Esculenta* – at the back of volume four). My focus was often drawn to the work's treatment of Liverpool, especially the photo of 'Liverpool from the air' (actually the Three Graces and the landing stage) in the chapter dealing with 'The Busy North'. I proudly read and re-read the imperative description: 'we have to think of Liverpool not only as a cotton and foodstuff port that is the headquarters of many of the leading steamship lines in our Homeland, especially those running regular services to Canada and the United States, to South America and the West Indies, and to West Africa'. One line I knew by heart: 'Liverpool's water-front is one of the wonders of the world'.

The Mersey once marked off Northumbria from Mercia, and later Lancashire from Cheshire, but borders are not simply physical – the river later became one of the dividing lines between Scousers and 'woollybacks' or 'wools' as the term later became (some of whom who lived 'over the water'). Where the railway crossed the Mersey at Widnes/Runcorn was the most significant boundary for me. By then the train to Oxford, and, later, Southampton (though I taught at Oxford, my first salaried job was at the University of Southampton) had passed our house in Lascelles Road; I could see it clearly and painfully from the window. As the train crossed the gleaming expanse of the Mersey below, and passed the blurred iron lattice of the rail bridge, slowing for Runcorn station, it meant that I was, again, embarking on the leaving of Liverpool, and it grieved me sorely. My father told me, the morning of his death, that he had often wept on the way back from Lime Street after he had dropped me off; I didn't tell him, though I wish I had, that often too, once past Runcorn, I had gone to the toilet and cried my eyes out. It took a very long time to escape from the sense of anxiety, loneliness and sadness that overwhelmed me on that journey, feelings that became unbearable once the train left Banbury (the last stop before Oxford). Of course I know the brutal cost of physical borders. I lived in San Diego for a while and travelled the twenty miles down to Tijuana in Mexico every so often. My privileged (white, Green-Card-holding) return to the United States through the militarized, high-tech, surveillance-controlled *frontera* was a lesson in the ways in which identity is constructed and policed by the state rather than chosen (try self-identifying as an American to La Migra if you're a Guatemalan refugee). The wall and all its attendant violence did its job. But there are invisible borders too – spatial borders, class borders, cultural borders, psychic borders ... borders that seem to be one-way, in the sense that, once crossed, you can return (which is part of the problem), but not quite to the same place, nor as the same self. Liverpool to Oxford is only 173 miles but, in whichever direction I was travelling, they were long, transformative miles.

Terminus was the Roman god of boundaries (from the Greek τέρμα, *térma*, 'end, boundary, limit'); his function was economic and political – to mark the boundaries of land possession. The terminus for us was the Pier Head – it was where all buses stopped and a two-minute walk to the landing stage and the Mersey. Occasionally, at Easter or in the summer holidays, we went and swung on the black border chains designed to stop us from falling into the treacherous river (while I was at secondary school, a distant relative, unloading a cargo boat, fell into the docks; we feared death by water, but he died of tetanus). We waited for one of the ferries – the *Royal Iris* (known as the 'fish and chip boat'), *Royal Daffodil*, *Woodchurch*, *Egremont* (the last two, refurbished and renamed as *The Royal Iris of the Mersey* and *Snowdrop*, are now the remaining ferry boats); squat, black and white, they swung before coming sideways onto the lanny, squashing the huge tyres used as buffers. The rattle of the chains as they lowered the boarding ramps was the signal for a mad rush to try to get seats upstairs, the best 'spec' to see Liverpool receding behind us. The favoured destination was New Brighton, which featured an outdoor, horribly cold, salt-water swimming pool with slides, a row of cafés (the Ham and Egg Parade), and possibly the dirtiest beach in

Britain (not for nothing was the Mersey called 'shit creek'). Salmon paste butties, for which I have retained a comfort food taste, were the order of the day; there are salmon in the river now.

The boundary between the Mersey and the Irish sea, and thus the entrance to the waterways of the world, is marked, more or less, on Crosby beach, by 100 cast iron figures of a naked man. Sculpted by Anthony Gormley, they embody the harmony and conflict between nature and culture as they rust, silt up, are barnacled, disappear and reappear with the tide ('tide' encompasses the natural and cultural in its dual meanings of 'ebb and flood of the sea' and 'segment of time'). Aptly enough, given its location and the gaze of the figures out to sea, the work, though known locally as 'The Iron Men', is entitled 'Another Place'. As a child, I wondered about those other places that the river opened up, or at least those I knew about from talk and my imperial reading: Birkenhead, the Isle of Man, Belfast, Dublin, the West Indies, Africa, India, South America, the United States, Canada ... And I lay awake at night – in Prophet Street, Lascelles Road, Stormont Road – listening to the fog horns and ships' sirens, excited at the promise of mist in the morning, tingling with expectation at the prospect of Bommie night and Christmas, thinking of ships and travel to faraway places. Happy and ignorant as yet of the forced crossing of boundaries that lay at the heart of the bitter history of slavery and diaspora that the river Mersey also helped deliver to the world, part of whose legacy is the architectural splendour of sections of Liverpool's city centre and waterfront. This is the river that provided the pelf, stolen by stealth, that created the wealth ....

NARK

There I was reading, minding my own business one evening in late September 2018, when I happened to look down at my phone. There were a number of messages and, as it turned out, emails, some of which were marked urgent. So I had a look and, lo and behold, a number of people, including several colleagues, wanted to tell me something very important indeed: my *Liverpool English Dictionary* (2017) had featured in that evening's episode of *The Great British Bake Off*. I'd never seen *Bake Off*, but I found the latest episode and there it was – Noel Fielding and Sandy Toksvig were reading the *LED*. In fact, they were looking up a word to describe one of the judges on the programme, Paul Hollywood, a Liverpudlian (well actually, he was born in Wallasey, so technically he is a woollyback, but there it is). Now there were a number of things I could discuss – the TV-watching habits of academics, for example, or the effect that popular culture can have on perceptions of scholarship (universities now call this 'impact', which was the word we used to use when talking about car crashes) – but instead I'll focus on the word that they found in the *LED*: 'nark'.

The principal task of lexicography – or dictionary-making – is the classification of words and their meanings. This can be a laborious and time-consuming undertaking, as the history of the *Oxford English Dictionary* shows: the *New English Dictionary* (its original title) began effectively in the late 1850s, with the first volume published in 1888, and the final volume in 1928. A 'Supplement' appeared in 1933 to accompany the full twelve-volume edition – then called the *Oxford English Dictionary* – and further supplements were published until the appearance of the second, twenty-volume edition in 1989. The third edition was started in 2000 and will never be printed – it will be a fully electronic resource. The good and bad news for lexicographers is that, simply because of the historical nature of language – its flexibility and thus variability – no dictionary is ever finished. If you're looking for a job for life, dictionary-making is worth a thought.

Even simple words can be difficult for the lexicographer. The verb 'to run', for example, has 645 meanings (over seventy-five columns of type in the *OED*'s printed second edition) – as in ... well, never mind. Words that have different meanings are described as polysemous (though it's difficult to think of a word that, in a specific context, cannot have different meanings). And sorting through and separating the meanings can be problematic, to say nothing of the labour involved in finding quotations to illustrate the different senses of a term. This is considered important in lexicography since it serves as evidence that the word is attested and that the interpretation is correct. For that reason, I used the *OED* methodology in the *LED*, though it did lead to certain problems, principally the difficulty of 'scriptism' – which amounts in effect to saying that if a word is not recorded in written form, then it isn't a word. For example, I know that the word 'mogger' exists, because I used it when I was a child, but I didn't have a written source for it and thus it couldn't be included in the *LED*. It wasn't the only example.

'Nark' is an interesting example of a complicated Liverpool English word. It is both a homophone (all of its instantiations are pronounced the same) and a homograph (it is always spelled the same). As a noun, it has four distinct meanings, as can be seen from the sentence: 'that nark[1] was in a nark[2] and that made him have a nark[3] with that nark[4]'. Let me tease the senses out in turn. 'Nark'[1], 'an argumentative, annoying person', as in 'a little nark, who was called Sir Stanley Grouse' (Jacques 1977: n.p.); it was recorded in Liverpool English from the mid twentieth century, and the derivation is probably from a northern vernacular verb, recorded from the late nineteenth century, 'to nark', 'to vex, annoy, irritate'. 'Nark'[2] refers to 'a state of anger, irritation', as in 'not hardened junkies, when deprived of dope,/Ere felt such anger, ere got such a nark/As a Scouseville driver seeking space to park' (Moloney 1966: 51). This was another mid twentieth-century coinage, though before its appearance in the *LED*, this sense was unrecorded (it has been included in the latest – June 2022 – revision of the *OED* entry); the derivation is probably an extension of 'nark'[1]. 'Nark'[3] means 'an argument', as in 'a family nark then was started' (Jacques 1975: n.p.); this also dates to the mid twentieth century, and again the derivation is probably from 'nark'[1]. 'Nark'[4], however, is significantly distinct; it means 'an informer' – as in 'the person next door could think they were a copper's nark' (McClure 1980: 115); recorded from the mid nineteenth century, the term has no apparent connection to 'nark'[1], and derived from Romani *nak*, 'nose'.

One of the ironies about lexicography is that the difficulties in ascertaining meaning that the dictionary-maker has don't necessarily seem to afflict the everyday language user. Consider these verbal examples: 'cod on[1] that he didn't cod on[2] to us'; 'let on[1] to him that she was only letting on[2] that she knew them by letting on[3]'. These sentences might raise a smile, because they are jokey plays on words, but they are comprehensible. They could be paraphrased as: 'pretend that he didn't acknowledge us' and 'tell him that she was only pretending to know them by saying hello'. For the lexicographer, on the other hand, the words present problems of recognition and classification, definition, and supporting evidence. 'Cod on' is tricky. 'Cod on'[1] means 'to pretend, joke with, fool someone', as in 'cod on yer don't know!' (O'Hanri 1950: 2); recorded from the mid nineteenth century, in the sense of 'to hoax, to take a "rise" out of', it appears to be an extension of a seventeenth-century cant term 'cod', 'a fool', which was a pejoration of the slightly earlier 'cod', 'friend or companion'. 'Cod on'[2] is even more complicated; meaning 'to acknowledge', as in ''e wooden cod on wen I waned mugging, aldo I was skint' (Whittington-Egan 1955b: 216), the derivation is unclear (it doesn't seem related to 'cod'[1]) and the term is not recorded in the *OED*. 'Let on' is similarly difficult. 'Let on'[1], 'to reveal, divulge', as in 'it's no use letting on we're beat, is it?' (Hanley 2009 [1950]: 286), is recorded in the *OED* from the early eighteenth century and glossed as 'dialectal' (in fact it is Scots). 'Let on'[2], 'to pretend', as in 'he had let on to the people at home that he was still working' (Hanley 1932: 79), is recorded in the *OED* from the early nineteenth century and again classed as 'dialectal' (and later, an 'Americanism'), whereas Jamieson's *Etymological Dictionary of the Scottish Language* (1808) indicates it is a medieval Scots term whose derivation is unclear. 'Let on'[3], 'to acknowledge someone; say hello', as in 'don't be letting on' (Hanley 1932: 69), is unrecorded in the *OED*; it may be an extension of 'let on'[1].

There are, of course, limits. The sentence – 'listen mush[1], see that mush[2] over there, he's a mush[3] and he's just given that fella a smack in the mush[4] so they're taking him to the mush[5]' – would puzzle anyone. In this example, there are five distinct meanings for 'mush'. 'Mush'[1] is 'a general term of address; man, mate', as in '"understand, though, mush," he warned; "turn up late any more an' you've 'ad it"' (Cross 1951: 39); recorded from the early twentieth century, it derives from Romani *mush, musha*, 'man'. 'Mush'[2] means 'a stranger, outsider', as in ''e's a mush. *He is a stranger*' (Shaw 1966a: 29); recorded from the mid twentieth century, the derivation is unknown. 'Mush'[3] refers to 'a prostitute's client', as in 'she was fed up being pestered by the mushes every time she went out' (McClure 1980: 133); recorded from the late twentieth century and glossed by the *OED* as used specifically in Liverpool, it is probably an extension of 'mush'[1]. 'Mush'[4] signifies 'mouth, lower face', as in 'better than a smack in the mush' (Bryan 2003: 78); recorded from the late eighteenth century, the derivation is unclear, but it is probably from the northern vernacular 'muss', 'mouth'. 'Mush'[5] means 'police-station, Bridewell', as in 'someone had said I was mushed' (Clerk 1971: 43); recorded from the early twentieth century, this is an extension of late nineteenth-century Forces usage, 'mush', 'guardroom or military prison'.

Bill Labov, one of the most important sociolinguists of the twentieth century, once observed that the study of language as it is used in everyday life shows that all languages and dialects have the capacity to describe the world as it is. What the study of language in everyday use also shows us is that languages and dialects (or vernaculars as I prefer to say), are multifaceted, intricate, developing forms that serve the needs of their speakers. Liverpool English is such a form, as the multiaccentual signifying capacity of terms such as 'nark', 'cod on', 'let on' and 'mush' show.

Let me be clear though: I've no idea whether 'nark' accurately describes Paul Hollywood or not. He seems like a perfectly nice woollyback baker to me (I use the word in its technical rather than pejorative sense – no insult intended, mush).

OLLIES

Morning in the City was an important documentary shown on BBC1 in March 1959, which focused on the realities – poverty, housing conditions, unemployment – of urban life in Liverpool, Manchester, Salford and Stockport. The film was the counterpart of *The Talking Streets*, broadcast on BBC radio in October 1958 (some of the soundtrack of *Talking* was reused in *Morning*). The documentary is a brutal but accurate representation of the conditions in which working-class people lived (as opposed to the sanitized version presented in *Coronation Street*, which began in 1960). As well as the difficulties of working-class life, however, *Morning* also depicted some forms of leisure. One scene, for example, filmed in the Dingle (Park Street – around the corner from Prophet Street), shows men playing ollies – known elsewhere as marbles; you can hear the clunk of the ollies as they hit each other. Writing later of his collaboration on *Morning* with Dennis Mitchell, the pioneering film-maker, Frank Shaw reported that a Liverpool councillor took them to see 'the specially made olly holes, half a century old, in his South End constituency' (Shaw 1966b: 4). Earlier evidence of the popularity of the game is furnished in *Owen Rees*, one of a number of late nineteenth-century Liverpool Welsh novels, in which the narrator observes: 'How convenient the court was to play marbles in from "ring taw" to "three holes"' (Roberts 1893: 9). Given that the courts – tenement houses grouped around a square yard – were notoriously impoverished, filthy, exploitative slums, this was a Pollyannaish if nonetheless true observation.

The popularity of ollies with men is puzzling at first sight, but there was perhaps a reason for it. My dad told me that ollies could be used as a form of gambling, when pitch and toss – the preferred form of street gambling – became too dangerous (it was heavily policed). 'Bang off', 'buttons', 'flemings' and 'jigs' were hybrid versions of both games. Street betting more or less disappeared following the legalization of most forms of gambling in 1960, after which you could lose your money in the discomfort of a smoky, litter-strewn bookies (the book was for calculating and recording the profits the bookie raked in), listening to the races blaring down 'the blower'. I worked as a counter clerk in Josie Jennings, the bookies on James Street, Garston, in the summer before university (£4 on weekdays, £5 on Saturday); it was a dispiriting experience, watching the male procession from Josie's to The Duck (officially The Swan) next door, and back again. My dad was an inveterate gambler; when he came to stay with me in New York, we went down to Atlantic City on the bus. They gave you $5 in quarters to get you started, but as we walked into an enormous casino he said to me, laughing: 'all you can hear is people winning, you can't hear anyone losing'. And it was true – all you heard was the slot machines paying out a few dollars in coins that hit the tin receptacles with a resounding sound. Anyway, we split up and agreed to meet in a couple of hours. He was very pleased with himself – he'd won 'good style' playing craps and suggested we go to dinner. As we tucked into steak and chips, the favoured celebratory meal, he asked me how I'd got on. Showing him the roll of quarters that I'd been given, I told him that I hadn't bothered. He was appalled; 'you are a disgrace', he said, 'and no son of mine – leave that money as the tip'. Anyway, his habit, and my experience at Josie's, cured me of any interest in gambling. It was the emotional investment (as well as the losses) that scared me off; heartbreak or ecstasy every half hour. Now you can sit in front of a screen and lose all the money that you don't have on a credit card gambling on sports in which you have no interest ('and the result of the Swedish under-16s volleyball semi-final is ...'); a corrupt game if ever there was one.

Ollies then were a serious business in Liverpool though for an older generation they were often played with 'cherrywobs' or 'cherrybobs' – cherry stones. The game produced a specialized vocabulary over time: 'bogies', 'bloody alley', 'glannies', 'jacks' (a larger ollie), 'lassies/lazzies', 'nunks', 'parrots', 'segs', 'ups'. We didn't use those terms, but ours were related: 'bloodies' (bright red); 'colourdees' (multi-coloured); 'greenie' (and 'yellowee', 'bluey' ...); 'oner' (an olly that had won one game, hence 'twoer', 'threeer' and so on – we played a lot, but even so, claims of a 'hundreder' were met with disdain); 'stonies'; 'steelies'. 'Steelies' were prized and so the fire that destroyed a local engineering factory but supplied us with 'steelies' of all sizes (otherwise known as ball bearings) was greeted with much glee. Mrs Gregson, our next-door neighbour, came to the gate warning us that the police would be round to collect them all back; we laughed, though we became slightly more circumspect about showing off our prizes. There were no flat surfaces for ollies; part of the fun of the game was making a perfectly calculated roll, with the ollie navigating bumps and dents in the road's surface to land up right next to the jack (or not).

There were plenty of other games that we played in the street, though the nostalgic view that kids in the past played out creatively all the time, whereas kids today are stuck indoors looking at screens, is surely dubious. Only some kids played out all the time (this was largely related to class – I went to secondary school with plenty of kids whose parents didn't let them play in the street because it was – dread word – 'common'). And those who did spent a lot of time hanging round being bored. Of course, we didn't play many of the games that our parents played. 'Tip cat', 'knurr and spell', and 'peggy', for example, were all variants of a game that involved throwing a small piece of wood in the air and then smashing it as far as possible (it was more fun to play, apparently, than to describe). But they'd gone by the time we were kids, as had 'flinchers' – a handball game in which the ball was thrown against the wall for someone to 'cop' (they played a version of this at Oxford – Eton Fives – I wasn't tempted) – and 'pannymug' – 'jacks' played with the remains of a broken cooking pot (the 'panmug'). Anyone's childhood games will be special to them because they are, in a deep sense, formative of our subjective and social identity, but it will hardly do to fetishize them. Walk past any school playground today and you'll see kids playing all sorts of games – some of which we played, some of which we didn't, though the basics are much the same. Games change their names ('heavy on ton weight' is now known as 'piley on'), but children play.

Given that I had a working-class childhood, I did play out a lot – there wasn't that much to do at home, and there wasn't even much telly on the telly. Footy or 'togger' was the most popular, of course; it was strictly gendered and excluded girls. Girls skipped and did so with a facility unknown to boys – except boys who boxed (which meant that nobody laughed at skipping). Skipping songs were plentiful: 'Call in my very best friend, my very best friend'; 'Johnny Todd, he took a notion'; 'On a mountain, stands a lady, who she is I do not know'; 'The big ship sails through the alley alley oh'; 'It's raining it's pouring'; 'One, two, three, alairy' ('alairy' is an etymological mystery). Just occasionally, outside a factory at dinner time, you'd see women skipping and smoking. Other games were played by everyone, and favourites included 'tick' (some called it 'golly', or 'shammy round the block', though it's more universally known as 'tag') and 'kerby', which involved trying to throw the ball from one side of the road to bounce on the kerb opposite back to you (a refined skill requiring hours of practice – if you bumped the ball off the edge of the kerb and caught it as it rebounded, you got double points). 'Tick' was linguistically interesting though because it featured the word 'barley' (uttered when you wanted to opt out of the game with impunity for a while – usually accompanied by the crossing of fingers). The term is recorded in the late fourteenth century poem *Sir Gawain and the Green Knight*, which was set in part near Liverpool (it mentions 'the wyldrenesse of Wyrale' – 'the woolybackdom of Wirral' in modern English) and written in the West Midland dialect of Middle English (whose provenance included part of Lancashire and Cheshire):

> And I schal stonde hym a strok, stif on þis flet,
> Ellez þou wyl diȝt me þe dom to dele hym an oþer
> barlay,
> And ȝet gif hym respite,
> A twelmonyth and a day.
> (Tolkien and Gordon 1967: 9, ll.294–8)

> (And I will take a blow from him right now on this floor
> As long as you give me the right to return it,
> By law,
> Though I'll let him off
> For twelve months and a day.)
> (my translation)

'Barlay' is possibly a pun here, playing on both *par loi* ('by law') and *parler* ('to speak' and hence 'truce'); our 'barley' – a respite governed by convention – had deep historical roots. The real favourites though were 'allyoh' (properly known as 'relalio', but also known as 'rallyoh', and 'relievo') and 'kick the can' – which was really just another version of 'allyoh'. The aim was for one person, or team, to guard the base and capture members of the opposing team, while the other team tried to avoid capture and set any captives free by kicking the can that sat on the base. Our base was invariably at the end of Prophet Street, where it abutted Gaskell Street, and the boundaries were clear: you couldn't cross Park Road, Northumberland Street, or Hughson Street. For the running team, the escape routes were numerous: over the wall into the back of the tennies (tenements) on Essex Street (home territory for me – my paternal grandparents lived there, opposite our house on the corner of Prophet Street) and through to Northumberland Street; or down to Essex Street and through the jigger on the left, behind our house, to Hughson Street; or down to Fernie Street and the jiggers that bordered the debby; or up to the left of the tennies on Gaskell Street and over the wall into Park Road; or up along Gaskell Street and over the wall and railings into St Winefrides. This last route wasn't the happiest for me; on one occasion, standing on the railings turning to descend backwards, I caught my trousers and fell forwards, smashing my face against the lower wall. Suspended by the ripped cloth, hanging upside down with my nose and mouth filling rapidly with blood, I heard the voice of the old woman who lived in the nearest ground floor flat: 'What have youse been told about climbing? Look at the state of you'. Her son rescued me from sanguinary drowning by lifting me off the railings and carrying me home, whence I was dispatched to the Southern Hospital (the Sudden we all called it, though it was anything but – we were there all day before I was told by a doctor that I had broken my nose and was lucky not to have lost my teeth). You could be too good at 'allyoh'. More than once I returned to base after a long excursion scurrying through jiggers and dodging through the tennies only to find that everyone else had long since gone home for their tea. It was scarcely worth kicking the can.

Anyway, ollies: 'olly' has been claimed to be a corruption of 'alley' ('jigger' as we called it), but in fact it is a plazzymorph of 'alabaster'. First recorded in the early eighteenth century, 'alley' meant a high quality 'marble', a term coined slightly earlier in the late seventeenth century (you can see children playing marbles in Pieter Brueghel's 1560 painting *Children's Games* – though the game itself is ancient). But as well as its plazzymorphism, 'olly' is an interesting term in that it exemplifies various types of semantic change. For example, 'ollies', presumably by dint of their shape, underwent metaphoric extension to mean 'testicles'. 'Ollies' also became idiomatic: 'your ollie's down the grid' meant you were in a hopeless position, while 'losing your ollies' (by analogy with 'losing your marbles') meant going mad. Of course, if your ollie *was* down the grid, that could well make you lose your ollies. It was a serious business.

PRODDYDOG

'Proddy dog' and 'proddy' meant 'Protestant', a term coined in the sixteenth century to refer to those 'protesting' against Papal authority (Latin *prōtestāns*, present participle of *prōtestārī*, 'to protest', root meaning 'to testify, bear witness', from *testis*, 'witness'). 'Proddy dog' pre-dates 'Proddy' and the earliest recorded usage is from the 1950s, though Anthony Burgess recalled the term from his Manchester Irish childhood:

> Cat lick, cat lick, going to mass,
> Riding to hell on the devil's ass.
> ...
> Proddydog, proddy dog on the wall,
> A small raw spud will feed you all.
> A ha'penny candle will give you light
> To read the Bible of a Sunday night.
> (Burgess 2012: 29)

As this suggests, 'Proddy dog' and 'proddy' were probably imported from Irish English or perhaps Scottish English. The derivation is unclear, but it may simply be based on a contrast with the pronunciation of 'Catholic' as 'Catlick' ('dog' as opposed to 'cat').

Though I was raised unequivocally on the Catholic side of 'the sectarian divide', my childhood use of 'Proddy dog' was slightly complicated by the fact that my mother's side of the family was Protestant. They were Merediths, from South Wales originally, so they might have been expected to be Low Church or Nonconformist, though they never showed much interest in religion at all as far as I could tell (well, except for Great Uncle Joey, who was a Jehovah's Witness, and both sides were united in finding that unnecessarily zealous). In fact there was a further complexity. My maternal grandfather, whom I never met (he died of tuberculosis before I was born, although I was informed as a child that he was swept overboard at sea – tuberculosis still being associated with poverty and uncleanliness in the 1960s), was apparently Catholic. I was told repeatedly, and naturally believed, that I was named after him; it was slightly disturbing then to discover, when we buried my grandmother, that his name was actually Vincent (further probing revealed that his nickname was Tony). Perhaps this reveals little other than the treacherous nature of family stories; pictures drawn on layers of tissue paper being tugged by different hands. In any case, I was in one sense the product of two mixed marriages – between my maternal grandparents and my parents. My father's solemn verdict on the topic was that mixed marriages don't work; 'men and women', he opined sagely, 'it never works'.

Anyway, mixed the background may have been, but Catholic we undoubtedly were: churched at St Malachy's, St Patrick's, Mount Carmel, St Francis of Assisi, St Bernadette's, schooled at St Malachy's, St Francis of Assisi, and St Edward's College). My own experience of religious difference as a child manifested itself in relation to education and some recreational activities (the Cubs and Scouts seemed very Protestant to me; I went once and there was a picture of the Queen on the wall, and that was the end of that). And then, of course, there was the Orange Lodge. We were warned strictly to 'go *nowhere near* them' (italics go *nowhere near* conveying the vehemence with which this prohibition was issued), so needless to say we went to see them whenever we could when they were 'out'. It was, after all, a marching band and, as well as the flutes and drums, there was lots of colour, and banners, and people dressed up. But even as a kid I could recognize the organized antagonism and the intense, eyes to the front, pseudo-militaristic order of the day. There were others on 'our' side who took exception to the Lodge's perambulations and confrontations were hardly unknown, especially in the Dingle and around Scotland Road; 'pepper-thrower' was one of the older terms for Catholics.

Sectarian antagonism in Liverpool ran deep and it is one of only a few major British cities – Belfast and Glasgow being the others – in which locals would recognize the meaning of the phrase 'The Twelfth'. It referred to the celebration of the Battle of the Boyne in 1690 in which William of Orange defeated the Catholic James II and established the Protestant ascendancy in Britain and Ireland; it afforded 'civil and religious liberty' to Established Church Protestants (though not Catholics or Dissenters such as Presbyterians). In nineteenth-century Liverpool English, 'The Twelfth' was also known as 'Carpenter's Day', from the preponderance of ships' carpenters in the Orange Lodges (an example of the long-lasting association between types of employment and sectarian affiliation in the city). 'Orange' is taken from King William's title, 'Prince of Orange', which originally derived from the Principality of Orange, a medieval feudal state in France (the commune of Orange still exists in Provence), rather than the colour, though they later became conflated. Hence the common early twentieth-century challenge 'I or O?', meaning 'Irish [Catholic] or Orange?', along with the later 'the Orange and the Green'. 'Orange Lodger', and 'Orangeman/woman', were other Liverpool synonyms for 'Protestant', as were 'Billy Boys' and 'Billies' (shortened forms of William). Pat O'Mara's *The Autobiography of a Liverpool Irish Slummy* (1934) records the phrase 'the Orange River', to refer to the areas in Liverpool in which Protestants were in the majority. 'George Wiser' is another old term for 'Protestant'; it derives from the evangelical Pastor George Wise, founder of the Liverpool Protestant Party in 1903 to contest local council elections. It was King William who popularized gin in Britain; I suspect George might not have approved.

I remember visiting the houses of friends in the Dingle in which there were not only pictures of the Queen, but pennants commemorating the Ulster Defence Association or the Ulster Volunteer Force (often featuring a representation of a man in a peaked cap, green combat jacket and dark glasses) together with artefacts made by the 'LPOWs' (Loyalist Prisoners of War). 'Lest We Forget' was a slogan repeated so often on the kitchen kitscherie that it seemed that there was little danger of anyone not remembering whatever it was that they were supposed to recall (the power of the admonition was all the greater for its lack of specificity). I have thought many times since of those lines by Tom Paulin, the Northern Irish poet of Protestant Republican persuasion (there are a few): 'There is so little history, we must remember who we are' (Paulin 1983: 29). I can only presume he was being ironic.

Once I called for a friend down the street with whom I played every day in the summer. His mother appeared, and then suddenly, and very unusually, his father came to the door to deliver the message: 'he isn't playing with you today'. Illness, punishment, unexpected visitors? No, it was July 11th – the day before The Twelfth (though actually, if we must remember, the Battle of the Boyne took place on July 1st – Julian Calendar – the shift to the Gregorian Calendar in 1752 made it the 12th). In any case, it was the day before the Lodge's annual noisy and boozy trip to lah-di-dah Southport (I doubt if I have ever thought of, or said, the name 'Southport' without the modifier 'lah-di-dah' in front of it). No friendship that day then; play called off for a couple of days while history took its place. To his great credit, when we met years later after losing contact, my boyhood friend told me that he was ashamed of what had happened. 'Ah no problem' I said, and we drank and talked about something else. We were in the Orange Hall on Mill Street – Sam's as it was known (it took me a long time to work out that this was an acronym for Southern Area Memorial Hall rather than Sam someone or other who managed it). It was adorned with the same old pictures: Billy on his white horse from 1690; a glamorous Elizabeth II circa 1957; a Loyalist volunteer in his peaked cap from 1973. I was out with my dad who, despite his serious adherence to his own faith, drank occasionally in Orange Halls with one of his best friends – a 'staunch Orangeman' (was that phrase a compliment? And did he really drink 'vodka and orange' to make a point whenever I ordered the drinks?). I never felt uncomfortable in the Orange Halls, since they were full of people I'd grown up with, and there we were, me and my childhood friend, chatting away. I told him, dragging the topic in an unwanted direction, that I'd always felt slightly envious of Proddy-dogs when we were kids since they never seemed to have to do anything religious ('their' cathedral was usually empty; 'ours' was always full of people being baptized, making their first confession and first holy communion, being confirmed, getting married, being buried, celebrating the lives of saints, popes, archbishops, being told off by priests ...). On the other hand, they did always seem to have the burden of having to remember something.

I had one last personal encounter with the Liverpool Lodge. In October 1981, just after I had finished my undergraduate degree at Oxford and started a further degree in Comparative Philology and General Linguistics, the Oxford Orange Lodge decided to hold a service at the Martyrs' Memorial (just outside the back door of Balliol College, for which I played footy, and opposite the Taylorian Library, where I studied) and to parade around the city. The Lodge had organized in Oxford since 1964 (the local lodge was constituted by Ulstermen and Scots working at Cowley car works), but the occasion of this event was the 'Anti-Papal Visit Campaign', designed to thwart John Paul II's trip to Britain in 1982 (the first by a reigning pope). Liverpool's Orangemen organized a special train to Oxford to take part in the brethren's protest and one of them, an acquaintance of my father, assaulted a policeman, who obviously didn't understand the traditional rights of the marchers as he attempted to 'break' the parade by crossing the road through it. The cop was injured and the Orangeman was locked up. This was slightly fortunate for me as it turned out since I had arranged, out of deference to my dad, to meet some of his friends for a drink, but they were otherwise occupied trying to arrange bail. Despite all those injunctions to remember that I had seen and heard since my childhood, I just clean forgot.

One of the verses of the folk song 'In My Liverpool Home' observes that 'The Green and the Orange have battled for years/They've given us some laughs and they've given us some tears'. Sectarianism didn't give us many laughs, as far as I can remember, although the opening of the Catholic Cathedral (known officially as the Metropolitan Cathedral of Christ the King and unofficially, from its shape, as 'Paddy's Wigwam', 'the Mersey Funnel', or, to older speakers, 'Coggers' Circus') was the occasion of wit. 'God Bless our Pope 1967' was painted rather defiantly (given the local demographics) in large letters on a wall at the end of my grandparents' street in the Dingle. It was almost immediately amended to 'God Bless Our Popeye 1967', which I found amusing, and my grandfather really didn't. Talking of cathedrals, I told my dad when I was about thirteen that we'd been warned by one of the Christian Brothers at school not to go into Liverpool's other great cathedral – we have, as it happens, 'got one to spare' as the song says. Never one for the grand gesture, my father merely frowned and pursed his lips (signs of deep disapproval), but next Sunday afternoon found us wandering around the interior of the Anglican Cathedral (known officially as the Cathedral Church of the Risen Christ and unofficially as 'their' cathedral); building started in 1904 and was finally completed in 1978 – it is the last great Gothic cathedral in Europe. We went to the tomb of the Earl of Derby, where, hidden away on the sculpture, my dad showed us the figure of a small mouse that the sculptor had included in his work (now anachronistically called 'the scouse mouse'). We walked back to the central space, under the largest bell tower in the world, where we looked east and west at the beautiful windows in one of the masterpieces of modern British architecture. 'Imagine telling anyone that they couldn't see this', my father said pointedly. Imagine indeed.

Under the foundation stone of the Anglican Cathedral there is a time capsule hidden by Jim Larkin, Irish Republican Socialist, and Fred Bower, stonemason and socialist activist. Religious antagonists as kids in the Dingle (Larkin was Catholic, Bower Protestant), they became comrades in the Socialist Party, and took the opportunity presented by Bower's work on the Cathedral to bury a time capsule in the building's foundations containing an address to the future. It begins: 'To the finders! We, the wage slaves employed on the erection of this cathedral, to be dedicated to the worship of the unemployed Jewish carpenter, hail ye!', and continues to inform its readers that 'within a stone's throw from here, human beings are housed in slums not fit for swine' (Bowers 2015 [1936]: 78). The 'Kingdom of "God" or "Good" on Earth' that Larkin and Bowers prophesied has hardly been realized, yet, but the anti-sectarian sentiments that their friendship embodied are now dominant. Everyday sectarian discrimination has more or less died the death in Liverpool, though there are some die-hards left. Given its deep historical roots in the city, that's quite an achievement. The reasons for its decline are complicated, though they include the fact that a common Liverpool identity has displaced confessional affiliation: Proddylicks and Cattydogs, we're all Scousers now.

QUEG

There used to be a story about the British Victorians – that they were prudish, sexually repressed, and imposed a taboo on matters to do with the body (it is said that they invented the terms 'white meat' and 'dark meat' to avoid mentioning 'breast' or 'legs' and 'thighs'). It is a tale that persists in popular culture, often as part of an appeal to a set of conservative ideals. Margaret Thatcher proclaimed a return to 'Victorian values' in the 1990s, as did her successor John Major (though he called it 'back to basics'). But there's the official line, and then there's reality (a distinction exemplified when Major was revealed to have had an extended extra-marital affair with a fellow minister – 'back to bed' as the satirists said). Official Victorian culture may have presented a particular view of sex and sexuality, but it was rather belied, just to take one example, by the claim that prostitution was notoriously widespread in major British cities, particularly in port towns such as London and Liverpool. Besides which, what we now know of the Victorian period is that, far from imposing a tabooed silence, it saw the invention of a number of new forms of discourse that took sex and sexuality as their subject – legal, medical, popular-cultural, psychoanalytical and sexological. Liverpool made its own contribution to this dissemination of discourse and knowledge: the Museum of Anatomy (also known as the Museum of Sex), on Paradise Street, in the heart of Sailortown, operated for some forty years, before being closed down in 1874. The museum was 'open daily for GENTLEMEN, from 10am to 9pm ... For

LADIES, Tuesdays & Fridays 2 until 5pm', and as well as various anatomical displays, and with 'upwards of 1000 models and diagrams', the exhibition covered topics such as 'Masturbation, Hermaphrodites', 'Dissectable models of the Venus, Eve, Tight Lacing &c', and 'Onanism'. To illustrate the dangers of Onanism (from Onan, a Biblical masturbator or, in an alternative reading, practitioner of *coitus interruptus*), the exhibition presented a model of 'a young man whose blood became so impoverished as to produce emaciation and general decay' (he died aged twenty-six), and 'five models, depicting the disastrous effects of onanism in the female' (with the helpful note that 'females guilty of this habit usually abhor the opposite sex') (*Descriptive Catalogue* n.d.: 34). Sex and sexuality were framed, shaped, influenced, categorized, figured, represented, evaluated, prescribed and proscribed during the Victorian period. Repressed they definitely were not.

There was (and is) a developed vocabulary around sex and sexuality in Liverpool, including a plethora of terms for coition (usually based on a presumption of heterosexuality, frequently from a male perspective): 'to bag off', 'a bash', 'bayonet practice', 'a belt', 'to block', 'to blow through', 'to carry on', 'to cop off with', 'to get off with', 'to get your end away', 'to get your hole', 'to goose', 'to have it away', 'to have it off', 'to knock off', 'to knock a slice off' (Grose's 1787 *A Provincial Glossary* explains this as 'to intrigue; particularly with a married woman, because a slice of a cut loaf is not missed': Grose 1787: *s.v. slice*), 'to get your leg over', 'a screw', 'to screw', 'a shag', and 'to shag'. Other sexual activities were covered by 'blosh' and spreck up' (ejaculate), 'finger pie', 'jigger jerker' (presumably after an encounter with 'up the entry eyes'), 'kneetrembler', 'nosh' (fellatio), and 'squirreldance' (foreplay). 'Getting off at Edge Hill' referred to *coitus interruptus* (Edge Hill is the last stop before Lime Street, Liverpool's main railway station – it's where Onan always left the train), while 'gozzy' was the term for another form of contraception, a condom (though there was always the danger of the 'Welsh letter' – a condom with a leak). There were, of course, various words for the male and female genitalia (in addition to the common terms): terms for the vagina included 'blert', 'minge', 'jaxy'/'joxy', and 'snippet', while the penis was covered by 'dicky' (which also appeared in 'dicky dyke', 'toilet attendant', and 'dicky docker', this last meaning 'rabbi', from the fact that the rabbi 'docks' (trims) the 'dicky' (penis) during the Brit Milah ceremony – and 'Dicky Lewis'), 'dobber', 'mutton dagger', and 'nudger'; 'jocks' and 'ollies' referred to the testicles. Interestingly, Liverpool English also had a number of words for a reluctant (male) sexual partner: 'Father Christmas' (who comes but once a year); 'Jump Sunday' ('Jump Sunday' was an annual event held the week before the Grand National at Aintree – 'every Jump Sunday' means 'infrequently' with a play on 'jump', 'sexual intercourse'); 'yunnuck' (a corruption of 'eunuch').

Words and their histories can tell us much about the past. For example, Liverpool English had various terms for cohabitation – 'living jockey-bar' (a 'jockey-bar' is 'the flat bar at the top of a grate)', 'living over the brush' (supposedly a reference to part of a Romani marriage ceremony, when couples jump over a brush, though it may also be a legacy of slavery in the United States), and 'living tally' (possibly from a seventeenth-century meaning of 'tally', 'two corresponding parts that fit together'). So, at the very least, it is clear that cohabitation was practised, particularly among working-class communities. And yet the historical lessons from language are not always easy to understand. Earlier, for example, I referred to the claim that prostitution was widespread in Victorian Britain – one often cited assertion is that there were 80,000 prostitutes in London alone. But the problem with such claims is that the term 'prostitution' has not always meant what it narrowly means today (payment for sex). Consider the *OED* definition of 'prostitution' (revised in 2007): 'the practice or occupation of engaging in sexual activity with someone for payment; (in early use also more generally) licentiousness, lewdness, harlotry'. Evidently, the current meaning is clear, but what of the reference to earlier senses of 'licentiousness, lewdness, harlotry'? What did these terms mean? Historically, as the *OED* indicates, 'licentiousness' has meant the 'assumption of undue freedom; disregard of rule or correctness; laxity, looseness', as well as the 'disregard of law, morality, or propriety; outrageous conduct'; 'lewdness' is defined historically as 'ignorance; want of skill, knowledge, or good-breeding; foolishness', 'wickedness; evil behaviour', and er, 'lasciviousness'; 'harlot' was 'originally: a beggar, a vagabond. Later: a dishonest or unprincipled person; a scoundrel, a rogue (frequently as a term of abuse)' and later 'a female prostitute; (also) a mistress, a concubine. More generally: a wanton, lascivious, or sexually promiscuous woman. Also as a term of abuse or contempt for a woman'. Of course it is easy to become lost in the labyrinth of language here, but these definitions raise many historical questions in relation to normativity – legal, moral and social (note the continuing power of the vague term 'promiscuous' – how many partners can you have before being classed as 'promiscuous' exactly?). If prostitute was defined historically as 'any promiscuous woman, a harlot', and 'harlot' was defined as 'a mistress, a concubine', then perhaps our understanding of 'prostitution' when it refers to the past needs careful examination. To put the issue acutely, are women who were living jockey-bar/jockey/tally really to be classed as prostitutes?

Linguistic history and the pattern of categorization that it encodes can be difficult to untangle, but the language around sex and sexuality is always worth exploring, not simply in relation to the recording of specific issues, or the emergence of forms of classification, but also to the ways in which words can illustrate social attitudes and evaluations. One rather bizarre example of this process is the Liverpool English term 'cross-cut', used to refer to the putative shape of the genitalia of a Chinese or Jewish woman. Perhaps the least interesting aspect of this term is its factual inaccuracy, since its real significance lies in its role in the exoticization and pejorative representation of racial groups. Another example of the way in which words can reflect and in turn engender social attitudes is the extensive set of derogatory terms for women in English, of which Liverpool English has its fair share. 'Boys call "meal"', 'brass', 'business girl', 'charva', 'palliasse' and 'scrubber', are all terms that categorize women in terms of prostitution, though they usually refer to women who are sexually active (or, in truth, just any women). Other demeaning terms for women include 'bit of fluff', 'bit of meat' and 'bit of stuff', as well as 'bird', 'judy' and 'tart' (all of which can mean 'girl' or 'girlfriend', 'woman' or 'wife'). All of these terms are interesting historically. In the early fourteenth century, 'bird' meant both 'young man' and 'maiden, girl', though by the sixteenth century it had narrowed to mean both 'a prostitute, a promiscuous woman' and 'a young woman, a girlfriend, a mistress'; the common Liverpool sense, 'girl or woman', is probably an Americanism. 'Judy' is recorded from the early nineteenth century and is probably a reference to Judy, Punch's wife (originally called Joan, but changed to the eighteenth-century term 'Judy', meaning 'fool, simpleton'). 'Tart' is subject to some protestation. Frank Shaw claims that 'though the name has come to be a rather opprobrious one', in Liverpool the term has 'remained pleasant' (Shaw 1966a: 25); the *OED* reinforces this interpretation: 'applied, *gen[erally]* (orig[inally] often endearingly) to a girl or woman; freq. in Australia and N.Z. Also in Liverpool dial[ect]'). There are two arguments against this unlikely claim. The first is the fact that the *OED* also records 'tart' as a woman 'of immoral character; a prostitute. Also *loosely* as a term of abuse' (the two senses of 'tart' arise at more or less the same time – the mid nineteenth century). The second is the response of Liverpudlian women when men call them a 'tart'.

Perhaps the clearest examples of the embodiment of vicious historical attitudes to sex and sexuality in Liverpool English are the terms that refer to male same-sex desire and practice (no doubt the fear and hostility that lie behind this vocabulary is testament to both the dominance of hetero-sexual ideology and its fragility). Specific terms include 'back door job', 'bum boy', 'bum chum', 'cream poof', 'hom', 'nance'/'nancy' (from early nineteenth-century slang, 'nancy', meaning 'buttocks'), 'puff', 'punk', 'ship's Mary', 'shirtlifter', 'turd burglar', 'Wallasey lad', and 'yen'. Harshest of all is 'queg', which I've never heard said without contempt ('queg' is a plazzymorph from 'queer' – perhaps it's where Melville got the name for the character Queequeg in *Moby Dick*). These words, together with those that demean women, record and disseminate the values of a patriarchal and heteronormative ideology that categorizes any form of sexual difference from the dominant order as inferior and dangerous deviance. The good news is that many of those terms are disappearing as a result of a revolution around sex and sexuality that began, in historical terms, very recently indeed. It will be a long and complex revolution, difficult and hard-won, and the depth of the change that has begun is evinced by the antagonism that marks the debates. What gender, sex and sexuality will look like on the other side of the process, no one knows, though one thing is clear: whatever the new practices are, whatever the social categories and distinctions that lie in our future, they will be captured in language just as surely as those of the past and present can be found in our historical vocabulary, current or obsolete.

Oh, and the claim that the Victorians coined the terms 'white meat' and 'dark meat' to avoid mentioning 'breast' or 'legs' and 'thighs'? Not true I'm afraid. 'White meat' was used to refer to chicken and pork, as well as breast cuts of poultry, from the eighteenth century (it was an extension of a medieval term meaning 'food prepared from milk, dairy produce', originally from the Irish *bánbíd*). 'Dark meat' was a nineteenth-century Americanism and referred to mutton, venison and duck, as well as the legs and thighs of chickens and turkeys. In fact, somewhat predictably, both 'dark meat' (from the mid nineteenth century) and 'white meat' (from the mid twentieth century) were used as derogatory terms to refer to women as sexual objects. Ho hum, same old.

ROZZER

They were probably a bit busy, but if anyone in our house had read the *Liverpool Echo* on the day of my birth (at home), they would have noticed a front-page headline: '5 More men on Affray Charge'. Other items included 'Tunnel Traffic A Priority'; 'Family Escape in City Pub. Blaze' (notice the abbreviation of 'public house'); 'Miners' Pay Claim'; 'Footballers' Pay Proposals'; 'L'pool Stocks' (Liverpool still had a Stock Exchange); and 'Two Dogs In Russian Space Ship'. The weather outlook was 'showery, with a fresh wind'. If you read the front page of the *Echo* today (it doesn't matter which day), the weather forecast will probably be the same and it is more than likely that there will be an article on crime. Now, crime is integral to newspapers and rightly so because of its impact on the social fabric. But fear is a bestseller, and if you read the *Echo* on a regular basis you could be forgiven for thinking that Liverpool is a crime-infested disaster area run by gun-toting drug gangs (a perception also held by many outsiders who've never been to the city). Whereas, in fact, Liverpool is statistically a lot safer than London or Manchester and does well by comparison with similar-sized conurbations. Of course there is crime in Liverpool – it's a city – and some crime rates are relatively high – it's a student city and tourist destination with a flourishing night-life scene that revolves around drink – but crime-ridden it definitely isn't. On the other hand, Liverpool does have a panoply of terms for the police, some of which relate to the city's history as a major port, some of which are common elsewhere.

'Rozzer' is something of a mystery in terms of its derivation. It may be a plazzymorph for Sir Robert Peel, the founder of the London police force in 1829 and an Irish constabulary in 1814 ('peeler' is still a common term for the police in Ireland and Northern Ireland). But this is not the only etymological possibility. Another suggestion is that it may be from 'rousse' and 'roussin', nineteenth-century French slang terms for 'policeman', which were probably extensions from a slightly earlier sense of 'snitch' or 'informer' (supposedly from the fact that people with 'cheveux roux' – red-heads – were considered insincere and hypocritical). Or it may be from the Anglo-Romani term 'ruzlus', meaning 'strong', which seems possible given that Liverpool English also contained other Romani terms for the police: mingee (from 'mingri', 'policeman') and 'muskers' (from 'muskero'/'muskers', 'police' in general). A similar lack of clarity surrounds the term 'bobby', used in Liverpool and elsewhere, which is also thought to derive from Robert Peel. But an earlier possibility is given in Hotten's *A Dictionary of Modern Slang, Cant, and Vulgar Words*, in which he notes that 'the official square-keeper, who is always armed with a cane to drive away idle and disorderly urchins, has, time out of mind, been called by said urchins *Bobby the Beadle*' (Hotten 1860: s.v. *bobby*). In addition to which, Halliwell's *A Dictionary of Archaic and Provincial Words* (1847) indicates that 'bobby' meant 'to strike or hit', which is supported by the *OED*'s account of 'bob', meaning 'a blow', as well as 'a shilling' (hence the Liverpool kids' refrain: 'if your Bob doesn't give our Bob a bob, our Bob will give your Bob a bob in the eye'). 'Bobby', then, may have derived from Bobby the Beadle's practice of giving wrongdoers a bob. But if 'bobby' is now in general use, 'firebobby' seems unique to Liverpool; the derivation appears to be from the fact that when the Liverpool Fire Service was instituted in 1833, it was called the 'the Liverpool Fire Police'.

There are other less familiar names for the police. 'Basil' meant 'policeman' or 'fat man', though the derivation is unclear (Partridge's *A Dictionary of Slang and Unconventional English* rather unhelpfully says 'Liverpool: from before 1952': Partridge 1961: *s.v.* Basil). 'Gom', more abusive, was recorded in Andie Clerk's brutal memories of early twentieth-century street life, *Arab. A Liverpool Street Kid Remembers*: 'two goms came in and threw a drunken lascar over the rope' (Clerk 1971: v). Borrowed from Irish English, 'gom' was a shortening of the Irish *gamal*, 'lout, simpleton, fool'. Other less common terms were 'Paddy Kelly' and 'Paddy Riley', which referred to dock police officers (probably because a number of them were Irish); the docks of course had their own force. 'Slop', recorded in Hotten's slang dictionary, was probably back-slang ('esilop'). Last but not least, 'woollyback' began as an insult within the police.

Other terms are slightly more familiar. The 'busies'/'bizzies' is a general and non-offensive term for the police and derives simply from either 'busy' or 'busybody'; in context, it can mean non-uniformed officers, though the more usual terms for detectives are 'jack' or 'D' ('plainees' refers to the police in 'plain-clothes'). 'Cops' is now general in British and American English, though 'coppers' remains British. There are various suggestions as to the derivation; one version holds that 'cop' is short for 'constable on patrol', while another claims that it refers to the copper used to make the original badges of the London police. The most likely explanation, however, is the Northern vernacular verb 'to cop', meaning 'to capture, lay hold of, catch', though this may be a variant of 'to cap' recorded from the sixteenth century with the sense of 'to arrest'. If so, then the derivation may be from the Old French 'caper', ultimately Latin 'capere', 'to take, seize, capture'. The same root is the source for 'not much cop' (not much of a catch, not worth having), and 'cop on with' – older – and 'cop off with' – more recent (to meet, pair up with).

Fanciful etymologies are part of the fascination and fun of word histories, and even the most august sources are not immune to the temptation. For example, with reference to the 'lob' element of 'lobscouse' (the forerunner of 'scouse' – see the entry under 'Scouse'), the *OED* suggests for the etymology: 'perhaps onomatopoeic: compare the dialectal *lob* "to bubble while in process of boiling, said esp. of porridge"'. Aye perhaps; as I say to my students on my 'Key Words' course when we are considering etymology, 'if it says "perhaps", it means they don't know'. There is a good illustration of this tendency in explanations of the commonest word that we used when referring to the police when we were kids, and which is still retained: 'scuffers'. Hotten records 'scufter' as a 'North Country' term for policeman (Hotten 1860: *s.v. scufter*), though the origin of this mid to late nineteenth-century coinage is uncertain. There were, however, wonderful suggestions proposed in the pages of *The Liverpool Echo*. One gave the root as the Irish *gabh* (pronounced 'guv'), 'to take hold of, catch', hence 'gabhta', 'pronounced guffter' and thus 'scuffer' (O'Hanri 1950: 2) (note the dubious uses of 'hence' and 'thus'); while Frank Shaw suggested 'the German "scuffe"', meaning 'to throw off dust while walking' (Shaw appears to have made up the German verb) (Shaw 1950: 4). Perhaps the most ingenious etymological explanation was the claim that, after the Napoleonic Wars, redundant soldiers who had served in France joined local constabularies and adopted the name 'escoffier' – 'someone able and ready to "cook your goose" – taken from the name of Auguste Escoffier, the famous French chef and restaurateur' (Mistrolis 1964: 8). Sadly, as is often the case, the most plausible explanation for 'scuffer' is rather more prosaic. Francis Grose's *A Provincial Glossary, with a Collection of Local Proverbs, and Popular Superstitions* (1787) gives 'skuft' as 'the cuff or back of the neck', and adds 'scruff', 'the nape of the neck' in the second (1790) edition of his work; in both cases, the terms are classified as 'Northern'. In addition, in Scottish English, 'scuff' meant 'to hit with the flat of the hand, to strike with a glancing blow' (*Dictionary of the Scots Language* 2004: *s.v. scuff*). The likelihood is, therefore, that 'scuffer' is a blend of these terms and refers to a police officer 'copping' someone by the back of the neck, or otherwise hitting them, to enforce an arrest.

It was rare to see the police when I was growing up, and they were generally treated with wary suspicion and resentment. When they did turn up, usually mob-handed, it meant trouble. In general, most of my dealings with the cops were at Anfield, where, commonly, they used violence to control people they clearly regarded with contempt (this was before football became a middle-class sport in the 1990s). Riding horses into crowds, dragging and pushing people who didn't do as they were told immediately, using truncheons on fans who couldn't move, threatening and abusing us – anyone who attended footy in the 1970s and 1980s will be able to remember similar instances. Regulars at Anfield in the period will remember the police sergeants who walked around with their 'signalling sticks', a thick wooden stick tipped with metal (so-called because, before modern telecommunications, such sticks were used by the police in local areas to signal to each other); its modern purpose was more accurately described by its alternative name, a 'savager cane'. If football hooliganism was a problem in the 1970s and 1980s, then excessive police violence was its ugly counterpart. There is an evident need for a communally supported and impartial police service that prioritizes public safety and protection (my experience in Northern Ireland, where I've worked, on and off, for a long time, has convinced me of that). But we know, from hard experience, that the rozzers have shown themselves too often to be incompetent in their duty to protect and serve the public as a result of systemic prejudicial attitudes. The 'Toxteth' riots (Liverpudlians say 'Liverpool 8'), the Miners'

Strike, Hillsborough, the Stephen Lawrence murder investigation, collusion in Northern Ireland, and the Sarah Everard murder, are just a few examples of the abuse of police powers. Guaranteeing public safety is a crucial social function and, given that, in order to carry out that role, we entrust the police with the most terrifying capacity – the use of violence in order to arrest and detain – why would we not need (and the police themselves not want) transparency and accountability? Thomas Hobbes was the seventeenth-century theorist of the social contract on whose work so much contemporary commonsensical thinking about the authority of the state is built. But even Hobbes realized that the social contract was conditional; once broken, as the experience of Northern Ireland should have taught us, it can be very difficult to put it back together again.

I've had dealings with a number of peelers during my work in Northern Ireland; my favourite observation on the police was made by a senior officer one day in Belfast. Wryly, he remarked: 'only a relatively few situations can't be made more complicated and usually worse by calling 999'. A fair cop.

SCOUSE

We had scouse for tea on Monday nights, if we'd had beef or lamb with roast dinner the day before. We weren't the first, as 'Nautical Philosophy', an eighteenth-century English ballad, reveals: 'Some are rolling in riches, some's not worth a souse/Today we eat beef, and tomorrow's lobscouse' (Dibdin 1781: 194). For us, scouse was an everyday, cheap meal that made the most of left-over meat by cooking it up with onions, carrots, potatoes and oxo cubes (there was a poorer version, without the meat – 'blind scouse'). I was surprised to find that scouse wasn't eaten in other places, and I had to correct people at Oxford who insisted on telling me that it was 'just' Lancashire hot pot or Irish stew. The ingredients in all three dishes may be common, and there are no doubt variations wherever vegetables and meat are available ('loblolly' is another example), but whatever the merits of Lancashire hot pot and Irish stew, they weren't scouse. And 'scouse', the word, predates both 'Lancashire hot pot' and 'Irish stew' by a century or so, or at least its forerunner word, 'lobscouse', does. 'Lobscouse' was first recorded in Ned Ward's *The Wooden World Dissected* (1707), a satire on naval life, in which a 'sea-cook' is described: 'He has sent the Fellow a thousand times to the Devil, that first invented Lobscouse; but for that lewd Way of wasting Grease, he had grown as fat in purse as a *Portsmouth*-Alderman' (Ward 1707: 83). A 'lewd Way of wasting Grease' indicates the notoriously poor quality of the dish, which was mainly served to sailors on ships. But in this sense, at least, the meaning of 'lobscouse' departs from its etymological root. Though something of a mystery – suggestions range from 'lob's course' (a 'lob' was a bumpkin or lout) to 'couscous' (eaten by Liverpudlian soldiers in colonial wars) – the origin probably lies somewhere in the North Sea/Baltic region – Norwegian *lapskaus*, Danish *lapskaus*, German *labskaus*, Latvian *labskauss* – meaning 'good bowl'.

The question is, how did 'lobscouse' become an English word, and how did it become 'scouse'? Though the roots and routes of words are often complex, it seems likely that 'lobscouse' was a sea-born and sea-borne word. Given that, as Daniel Defoe tells us in his *A Tour Through the Whole Island of Great Britain* (1724–26), Liverpool sent ships transporting salt and coal 'to Norway, to Hamburg, and to the Baltick' (Defoe 2005: 541), it is probable that 'lobscouse' came to these shores by way of the North Sea and Baltic trade. But if that is how it arrived, how and when did it become 'scouse'? The answer appears to be that the shortened form appeared in Liverpool at the end of the eighteenth century (the *OED*'s first example is 1840, but that's too late). The evidence lies in Sir Frederic Morton Eden's *The State of the Poor: or, an History of the Labouring Classes in England, From the Conquest to the Present Period* (1797), in which he referred to a parochial report on food expenditure in the Liverpool workhouse in the early 1790s. Citing the 'weekly bill of fare', Eden noted that the inmates had 'lobscouse' on Tuesday, Thursday and Saturday. More significantly, he listed the ingredients as 'Beef, 101lbs. for scouse... 14 Measures potatoes for scouse Onions for ditto', thus confirming that the term 'lobscouse' had been subjected to Liverpudlian plazzymorphism (Eden 1797: II 336). Incidentally, Eden also furnished the first recipe for the dish: 'Lobscouse is beef cut in small pieces, and boiled with potatoes' (and presumably the onions that he mentions) (Eden 1797: II 334). There is no reference to oxo cubes.

Scouse shifted from the poor house to the houses of poor Liverpudlians; it became part of the staple diet and, later, an element in the city's cultural identity (you can buy scouse pies at Anfield these days – the phrase 'a lewd Way of wasting Grease' comes to mind). Which is presumably why Liverpudlians became known as 'Scousers', or 'Scouse', though the story is a bit more complicated than it first seems. In fact, the common name for people from Liverpool in the nineteenth century was 'Dicky Sam', and in the twentieth century, at least till the latter decades, it was 'Wacker' or 'Wack' (whose derivation is unclear, though it may be a combination of 'whack', 'to divide or share' and 'whack', short for 'paddy whack'). So how did Liverpudlians become Scousers? 'Scouse and Scouser', a feature in the *Liverpool Daily Post* during the Second World War, suggests the most obvious answer:

> An old Liverpool seafarer who has been familiar with the term 'scouser' for many years suggests that it actually does owe its origin to the stew or hot-pot colloquially known as 'scouse'. Years ago, of course, this 'scouse' was the main midday meal for seamen and dockers in Liverpool, and all the dockside public houses made it one of their specialities ... Many a time he has heard one seaman remark to a Merseyside man: 'Oh, you come from the place of scouse'. And from this it is only a short step to calling a Liverpool man a 'scouser'. (Postman 1942: 2)

Eric Partridge, the great twentieth-century collector of slang, who edited *Songs and Slang of the British Soldier 1914–1918* (1930) with John Brophy, the Liverpool novelist, supported this view and claimed that 'Scouse' and 'Scouseland' were 'nautical and (Liverpool) dockers' usage in the late nineteenth and early twentieth centuries (Partridge 1961: *s.v scouse*; *Scouseland*). Yet the story is not quite so simple. Writing of the early use of the term, a number of writers noted its pejorative sense. John Farrell, for example, one of the earliest writers on Liverpool English, commented that "'Scouse", the local stew, gave to native members of the armed Forces (N.C.O.s and men) the name "Scousers". This term is hardly ever used as a mark of affection' (Farrell 1950b: 4). Another recalled: 'I heard the unlovely term "Scouser" used, and I feel fairly certain it was a wartime affectionate mark of disrespect that crept into circulation via the Army' (Bindloss 1957: 6). And James Callaghan, writing of the inter-war years, asserted that when 'Scouse' was 'applied to an individual it meant that person was the lowest of the low, a remark often leading to bloodshed' (Callaghan 2011: 29). The reason for this negative emphasis is unclear, though it is telling that an editorial comment in the *Liverpool Daily Post* noted that 'whenever the term "scouser" originated, it seems to have crept into general use in the Scotland Road area of Liverpool after the First World War' (Editorial Comment 1957: 6). This is significant because it appears to indicate that when 'Scouse' or 'Scouser' were used within Liverpool, they were associated with one of the poorest areas of the city – the docklands of the North End.

Be that as it may, it is certainly clear that 'Scouse' and 'Scouser' were adopted during the Second World War in Forces' usage. An anonymous contributor to the *Liverpool Evening Express* stated plainly that 'the Army nickname for a Liverpool man is "Scouser" and the members of the "Scouser" club are his brothers' ('"Scousers " are all brothers' 1943: 2), while another writer noted that 'a member of the Royal Navy said to me the other day, "When any chap from Liverpool joins our ship, we immediately christen him Scouse"' (Hill 1945: 4). Yet it is striking that in these examples, the terms 'Scouse' and 'Scouser' are applied by outsiders to Liverpudlians, rather than epithets used by Liverpudlians themselves. This is perhaps unsurprising, given the negative associations of the terms within Liverpool that were noted above. But it also raises an important issue in terms of the dating of the acceptance of 'Scouse' and 'Scouser'. Writing of his National Service in the mid 1950s, Jim Elliott noted that, on one occasion, 'the Sergeant Major then said: "You're a scouser aren't you?" I had never heard the expression before' (Elliott 2006: 141). The point was reinforced a decade later in Sean Hignett's fascinating novelistic portrait of Liverpool 8, *A Picture to Hang on the Wall* (1966), in which one character asks: 'Have you ever heard anybody calling anybody else scouse?' (Hignett 1966: 90). Even Brian Jacques, professional Liverpudlian (and author of the *Redwall* series of children's books), commented in the 1970s that 'at present it is not in vogue to use the word "scouse" on Merseyside' (Jacques 1973: n.p.). All of which leads to the conclusion that the use of 'Scouse' and 'Scousers' as positive terms within the city ('We are not English We are Scouse' – as the banner at Anfield put it in 2007), is a very recent development indeed. Even then, there are many Liverpudlians who feel considerable ambivalence towards 'Scouse' and 'Scouser' (I include myself in the number), precisely because of the stereotypical and usually negative connotations of the terms. The priest who was 'the Master' of my college (did they really invent such titles for themselves, and did we really go along with it?) used to say condescendingly 'ah, here's young Scouser now', whenever he saw me, though the effect was rather spoiled by the fact that he pronounced it in a posh accent as 'Scouzer'. Mind you, he also called me Colin for three years.

Liverpool English, and specifically the Liverpool accent – or at least what is perceived as *the* Liverpool accent, since it is variable – has attracted opprobrium since the end of the nineteenth century (as noted in the introduction). Inhabitants of the city, however, experience Liverpool English differently: as a medium of identity and belonging. This was expressed, with particular reference to accent, by a correspondent to the *Liverpool Evening Express* during the Second World War: 'Once outside your hometown, your accent gives away your birthplace and, so far as the Liverpool accent is concerned, it will always be welcomed by some others of the company, for Liverpool has its representatives in every Corps of the British Army, from the Airborne and Commandos down to the "lowly" Pioneers' ('"Scousers " are all brothers' 1943: 2). This claim is significant in two ways. First, it is a relatively early record of a perception among Liverpudlians of their accent as a common means of recognition, identity and solidarity. And, second, it does not mention 'Scouse'. There is a reason for this: nobody referred to Liverpool English as 'Scouse' until 1950.

The earliest mention of 'Scouse' was in an article by Frank Shaw, 'Scouse Lingo – How it all began', in the *Liverpool Echo* in December 1950 (typically, given the recurrent trope of the decline of dialects, its birth notice coincided with its funeral rites – Richard Whittington-Egan proclaimed in 1955 that 'Liverpool dialect is dying out': Whittington-Egan 1955a: 6). Shaw's piece built on John Farrell's two detailed and highly informative articles earlier that year in the *Liverpool Daily Post* – 'About that Liverpool Accent (or Dialect)' and 'This Half-Secret Tongue of Liverpool'. And it was Shaw who went on to become a founder member of what he himself called 'the Scouse industry' (along with others such as Fritz Spiegl, Stan Kelly, Peter Moloney and Pete McGovern) (Shaw 1971: 237). A prolific writer (as well as entertainer, entrepreneur, Liverpool city councillor, folk anthropologist, and customs officer...), Shaw's output was often repetitious and limited in various ways, but it did include a number of significant pieces of work. He was, for example, the first writer to make a sustained attempt to use Liverpool English as literary medium in *The Scab* (1952), a one-act play of Liverpool working-class life set during the 1926 General Strike; he collected and recorded a series of 'Scouse Talks' (1957) for the Liverpool Central Library; he researched an early BBC documentary on Liverpool; he published a three-part study of Liverpool speech – 'Dialect of a Seaport' in the *Journal of the Lancashire Dialect Society* (1958–60); and he translated Biblical selections into Scouse (Shaw and Williams 1967). Most importantly, he authored *Lern Yerself Scouse*, volume 1 (1966a) (the material was collected by Shaw and edited by Fritz Spiegl). Though this was in some ways a horribly nostalgic and deeply misogynistic text compiled by amateurs, it was at least a serious essay at analysing an urban vernacular and, as such, marked a radical departure in the study of language in England. In contrast, English dialectology of the post-war period (primarily the *Survey of English Dialects* (1950–61) – precisely the period in which Shaw's pioneering work took place) focussed on rural England areas and took as its prime informants 'old men with good teeth' (old men because they were considered to be conservative language users, good teeth so that their pronunciation would be clear). It is a sharp difference. The *SED* studied the 'real England' of the English countryside, with a view to capturing the death of English dialects (the view of local vernaculars as 'heritage' is never far from this approach). Frank Shaw attempted to capture the anthropological complexity of a living, developing urban form of language.

Shaw was then, undoubtedly, a major contributor to the serious study of 'Scouse', yet he was also responsible for a distortion of the history of Liverpool English, which became, unfortunately, the dominant understanding of the form. For it was Shaw who formulated (on the basis of a misreading) an account of Liverpool English that essentially saw it as the combination of Lancashire dialect and the Irish English spoken by the refugees from the Great Famine/An Gorta Mór in Ireland between 1845 and 1849. Shaw's inaccurate reading of Liverpool's language story was influenced in part by a laudable desire to put the Irish back into a history from which they had largely been excluded by dint of the dominant forms of sectarianism. But his account led to a gross simplification of a complex and still barely understood development. I discussed the origins of Shaw's account in *Scouse: A Social and Cultural History* (Crowley 2012), so there is no point labouring it. Suffice it to say that Liverpool, a major port from the mid to late eighteenth century on, was a 'contact zone': a 'social space where cultures meet, clash and grapple with each other' (Pratt 1991: 34). Liverpool was a place where a whole variety of people mingled, including (to name but a number of the attested communities): African-Americans; Austrians; Basques; Chinese; Filipinos; Germans; Irish; Italians; Kru (West Africa); Lascars (India); Mongolians; Poles; Russians; Scots; Welsh (Belchem 2006: 311–20). One consequence of such cultural mergings and conflicts is the formation of new forms of language; in Liverpool that meant the emergence of Liverpool English. What evidence is there to support this theory? The vocabulary of Liverpool English itself is one source, since it serves as the repository of many words taken from all sorts of cultures, with which Liverpool has been in contact one way or another. Liverpool English includes items adopted from Afrikaans ('scoff'); American English ('ace'); Arabic ('akkers'); Australian English ('not much cop'); Cant ('kecks'); Chinese ('char'); Cornish ('scadge'); Danish ('kip'); Dutch ('mopus'); Fijian pidgin ('bullamacow'); Armed Forces usage ('doolally'); French ('barley'); Gaelic ('kaylied'); Guyanese Creole ('tonka'); Hindi ('dekko'); Irish English ('left-footer'); Italian ('carzy'); Lancashire dialect ('cob'); Latin ('cental'); Manx ('tanroagan'); nautical usage ('hard lines'); Persian ('bukshee'); Polari ('tusheroon'); Portuguese ('bacalhoa'); Romani ('dixie'); Scots ('ming'); Spanish ('alicant'); Turkish ('burgoo'); Urdu ('cushy'); Welsh ('bad breath'); Yiddish ('nosh'). Other evidence is more observational. Thomas De Quincey described Liverpool as a 'many-languaged town' (De Quincey 2000: II 228), while an early twentieth-century observer called it 'polyglottic', an 'ingathering of the representatives of all nations (cited in

Belchem 2006: 319). Culturally and linguistically, Liverpool was a complex place; the history of the city is therefore badly served by the simplistic notion that Liverpool English is the result of the combination of Lancashire dialect and Irish English.

Scouse, the linguistic form, was christened in 1950, and it has since made its way into the cultural imagination of Liverpudlians and their fellow British citizens; 'Scouse' is also the term used by professional linguists to refer to the language of Liverpool. Yet, as I make clear in the title of *The Liverpool English Dictionary 1850–2015*, 'Scouse' is not my preferred term for two reasons. First, because its representation in various forms of popular culture means that what people usually refer to as 'Scouse' is simply an accent associated with Liverpool rather than Liverpool English (it is easier for actors to mimic an accent rather than for writers to use what may be unfamiliar words and forms). This is compounded by the fact that linguists, with few exceptions, also focus on the pronunciation of the form (for research reasons, linguists make an analytical distinction between accent and dialect that is not based in experiential reality – you don't speak or hear an accent and a dialect separately). And, second, given that 'Scouse' usually does mean accent alone, and that the accent identified with Liverpool is highly stigmatized nationally (if not locally – see 'woollyback'), using the term often amounts to colluding with a reductive and negative understanding of language in Liverpool.

So: eat scouse, are Scouse, speak Scouse? It might be better put as: eat scouse (because many of us still do), are Liverpudlians, speak Liverpudlian English.

TOGS

'Togge', meaning 'coat', is found from the early eighteenth century and is a shortened form of the cant term 'togeman', first recorded in Thomas Harman's cant glossary, *A Caveat for Commen Cursetors* (1567): "'their Casters and Togemans" ... *A caster*, a cloke. *a togeman*, a cote' (Harman 1567: n.p.). Though Harman calls cant 'Peddelars Frenche' (a derogatory description), 'togge' is probably a direct borrowing from French: *toge*, 'gown', ultimately Latin *toga*. The plural form 'togs' appeared in the late eighteenth century, with the general sense of clothes. This usage is exemplified a little later, in *Oliver Twist* (1838); when Oliver is led to Fagin's den by the Artful Dodger, one of the boys exclaims 'Look at his togs, Fagin! ... Look at his togs! – superfine cloth' (Dickens 1985: 163). A further sense is recorded from the early nineteenth century in sailors' talk; in Melville's *Redburn*, Redburn regrets that his 'shore clothes, or "*long togs*," as the sailors call them, were but ill adapted to the life I now led' (Melville 1849: 97).

In Liverpool English, 'togs' usually meant 'swimming cozzy', though it could just mean 'kit' of any sort – cricket, running or footy (for which 'togger' was an alternative name). As in its wider historical use, the term also meant clothes in general; for example, in the injunction to Benny and Nelly to 'get on yer best togs', in Silas Hocking's *Her Benny* (1879), the novel that all Liverpool schoolchildren read (and some saw – a silent film version was released in 1920). There were words that I dreaded hearing from the teachers at St Francis of Assisi primary school: 'don't forget your togs tomorrow!' It meant that we were headed to Garston ('Gazzy') Baths the next day, in single file, led by a teacher, where some very perfunctory swimming lesson would take place – 'swim to the end' – and we would be left to shiver our way back to Earp Street (Burp Street of course) for our dinner (known to some as lunch). The return journey was marked by a compulsory stop at Caulfields, the pet shop, on the corner of James Street and Chapel Road; budgies by the score, stinking rabbits, and the occasional snake. The Baths were a Garston institution and in the late 1950s they hosted dances (they put boards over the pool); my mother and father met there. For those who lived in houses without a bathroom (there were plenty – I was born in one), the Baths had single booths where you could luxuriate – for a fixed period; Fridays were mad busy and the whole place reeked of the Brylcreem that the men used to queue up to buy from the dispensers on the wall (for 'the Brylcreem bounce'). There were other baths: 'Stebbie' was attached to the Upper Essex Street wash-house; the Steble Street sign featured an image of a finger pointing 'To the Baths'– it seemed like an order. And Sneddies had its own swimming pool (a wonder in those days, and a sign of the school's standing and aspiration), in which, cured of any interest in swimming by my experiences in Gazzy Baths, I doggy-paddled with the other landlubbers in the shallow end while the accomplished swimmers boistered past doing impressions of dolphins in pain (or the butterfly stroke as it was surely misnamed).

'Togs' were always a source of potential embarrassment. If you did forget your cozzie at Garston Baths, they lent you one (invariably the wrong size, sometimes ridiculously so) and you used a wet communal towel. But it was in the wider sense of the term ('clothes in general') that the real problems came. It is hard to over-state how much anxiety and social embarrassment school clothes caused. Of course, one argument for school uniform is that it levels social distinction (it is after all 'uniform'), but any poor kid understands all too well how class differences are woven into every stitch of clothing. Sneddies insisted on a very expensive bright purple blazer (with school badge and motto – 'Viriliter Age' – another injunction) and multicoloured striped tie, both of which had to be bought from the school. But the rest of the uniform, and shoes, provided ample means by which the ability to buy dearer and better quality 'gear' could be made very clear (Marks & Spencer versus Garston market was only the start of it). Sports 'togs' were difficult in their own ways, and caused me an occasion of humiliation. In the summer, you had to wear 'whites' to play cricket and the sound of the games teacher's voice reverberated across the playing fields –'where's yer whites?'. Whites? Where would we buy whites? Greenbergs was the answer, the naval outfitters on Park Lane, opposite Joseph Heap's Rice Mill, near the Docks. And so we went and bought a pair of bell-bottomed bright white kecks (Greenbergs specialized in such items), which contrasted ridiculously (people laughed) with the off-white, cream even, narrow-legged trousers in which everyone else took to the field. I wore them once and, to my dad's dismay, stained the knees grass-green (it meant we couldn't take them back). After that, I turned to athletics, and sprinted for the school in a pair of pumps until someone gave us hand-me-down running shoes. Adidas, red, with spikes; they almost fitted.

The stigma associated with clothes wasn't new; it is a recurring theme in working-class autobiographies, particularly those written by women. In the early twentieth century, it was common to see children dressed in 'police clothes', which were given to the children of the poorest by the police and much despised (they were distinctively cut to deter pawning). 'Martin Enries' was another term for either cheap or second-hand clothes (from the name of a textile manufacturer), often bought at 'Paddy's Market' in Great Homer Street, or one of the more local markets around the city. In his *Portrait of Liverpool* (1970), Howard Channon, a local journalist, reported that 'Sailors from Asian and African ports still make a beeline for Paddy's to buy secondhand togs' (Channon 1970: 120). That may have been the case. But going to school in clothes or shoes bought at Paddy's – or Greenbergs – invited the sort of stinging insult that had a deep capacity to humiliate and shame in ways that perhaps only the poor schoolchild understands. 'Kecks' was our common term for 'trousers'; it is a version of the cant term 'kicks', 'breeches', recorded at the end of the seventeenth century in *A New Dictionary of the Terms Ancient and Modern of the Canting Crew*: '*Tip us your Kicks, we'll have them as well as your Loure,* Pull off your Breeches, for we must have them as well as your Money' (B.E. 1699: n.p.). My experience with my white 'kecks', ended any interest I might have had in cricket; it was clearly not a game for us.

From at least the 1950s, Liverpool has been at the forefront of developments in popular culture. Its significance as a musical centre goes without saying, but it has also been an important location for fashion and style ('Cunard Yanks', sailors on the transatlantic routes, were an important conduit for American clothes). It should be no surprise, then, that a city as style-conscious as Liverpool has its own distinctive vocabulary related to clothes or dress-sense. Some terms came by way of naval or Forces' slang. A 'rig out' (or 'to rig someone out'), is from the seventeenth-century naval term 'to rig', 'to prepare a ship for sea', and the same source also produced the now obsolete 'snapper rigs' (old clothes). Other terms had much older roots. 'Gear', meaning 'clothes', dates from the fourteenth-century; John Gower's *Confessio Amantis* (1390) has 'clothen in the same gere' (dressed in the same gear), in reference to Achilles' mother dressing him as a woman (a boy way before his time) (Gower 1901: 28). In Liverpool English, the noun 'gear' became an adjective – 'gear' and 'the gear' – and was used in an adjectival phrase, 'it's the gear' – all of which meant 'good' or 'excellent' (*The Guardian* reported in 1963 that 'The Liverpool Sound ... put expressions like "it's the gear" into the mouths of debs': *Guardian* 1963: 9). The derivation is again probably early twentieth-century naval and Forces slang; *Soldier and Sailor Words and Phrases* (1925) records 'gear' as 'apparatus' (a sense that also dates to the fourteenth century), but notes that it is 'also used as a colloquial term for anything giving satisfaction – *e.g.*, "That's it, that's the gear!"' (Fraser and Gibbons 1925: 103). The dual meaning of 'clothes' and 'equipment' is also shared by another Liverpool term, 'clobber'; recorded from the late nineteenth century, the derivation is unknown.

Like most Liverpudlians, I'm happy to put on my 'bezzies' on suitable occasions (births, deaths, marriages and job interviews mostly), but I've never shared the general interest in clothes. In that regard, like my lack of interest in gambling, I am not my father's son, since he prided himself on being smart (any excuse to put on a jacket and tie – including a night in the pub) and I was a source of despair. Oddly, I was at home in the slovenliness of student life at Oxford, where casual dress was more or less the order of the day, though there were exceptions to that: we had to wear gowns for dinner and dark suits, white shirts and white bow ties for exams. Apart from that nonsense, the dress code was completely informal, as it is in my profession (one of the benefits of my job is that I don't have to dress up for work). I suppose I was conditioned by the circumstances of my upbringing in my attitude towards clothes, but perhaps not quite as explicitly as one of my students when I started teaching at my Oxford college. He turned up for the first tutorial in a brown tweed blazer, pale green tie, woollen checked shirt, green corduroys, and a pair of very expensive brown brogues. My greeting – 'I see you've got your bezzie togs on then' – provoked a stare of utter incomprehension that complemented my stare of utter disbelief. A culture clash, I suppose you could call it.

US

'Us' is a complex little word. Even its pronunciation is contentious. The *OED* gives /ʌs/, but that sounds like 'ass' to my ears and the common Liverpudlian pronunciation is /ʊs/ or /ʊz/. Given that /ʊs/ is also the sound used in most northern and midland areas of England, it might be wondered why the *OED* presents /ʌs/ as the way to pronounce 'us'? Comparison of the account given in the second (1989) and ongoing (digital) editions of the *OED* provides the answer. In the 1989 edition, the pronunciation guide notes simply that 'the pronunciations given are those in use in the educated speech of southern England (The so-called "Received Standard")'. As noted in the Introduction, the origins of this privileging of a particular form of speech (defined in terms of class and regionality) lie in the Renaissance, though its codification within the study of language began in the late eighteenth century and reached a high point in the early twentieth century with the extension of the term 'Standard English' to refer to speech (as opposed to its first use, as set out by the lexicographers who compiled the first edition of the *OED*, to refer to the historical norms and practices of the written language). The phrase 'Received Standard [English]', cited by the *OED* (1989), was coined by Henry Wyld, who, as I noted in the Introduction, believed that if you spoke with a Liverpudlian accent you could not be said 'to speak "good English" with perfect purity'. 'Received pronunciation', by the way, is said to be used by a tiny percentage of the population (estimates range between 2 and 5 per cent).

I did my doctorate on the history of the term and concept 'Standard English' and showed that the way in which the phrase had developed, away from its reference to writing to include speech, was confusing and damaging in language study, not least in terms of the education of children. This topic became significantly controversial in the 1990s, with the introduction of the National Curriculum in schools, and I spent a lot of time writing and campaigning to highlight the problems with the phrase 'Standard English' and the unfortunate consequences that can follow if it is not used with precision. I might as well have spent the time banging my head against a brick wall. The Tories, and then New Labour, embraced as prescriptive a form of the National Curriculum as they could get away with and, in my profession, linguists, particularly sociolinguists, often declared that my account of 'Standard English' was correct – but carried on using the term to refer to speech regardless. Over time, partly because of the dogged opposition of teachers to narrow conceptions of the language curriculum, partly because of the growing interest in language ideology, a more 'liberal', though still incoherent, view prevailed, which meant that 'Standard English' speech was taken as the 'correct' form (what else does the term 'standard' mean in this context?), but that other forms were permitted if they belonged to dialects or were used in informal speech. The tone of the change can be found in the guide to pronunciation found in the *OED*'s current digital form: 'The pronunciations given are those in use among educated urban speakers of standard English in Britain and the United States'. The 'standard' has now been extended to America – a reflection of contemporary linguistic power politics – and it is no longer confined to southern England but to cities (as opposed to rural areas presumably). And yet this formulation is in reality no less nonsensical than earlier versions. Is the claim really that 'educated speakers' in cities as diverse as London, Liverpool, Belfast and Edinburgh, or Los Angeles, Chicago, Houston and New York, speak with the same pronunciation? More pertinently, perhaps, since the issue has long dogged these debates, how 'educated' do you have to be before your pronunciation counts as that of an educated speaker? High school (any high school)? Degree level? My judgment is that the imprecision in the definition of 'educated' is simply a way of avoiding reference to class, but the class-based evaluation is still there. The reformulations can be as complex or as deceptively simple as they like, but they can't hide the fact that what is happening in these definitions is the selection of one form of pronunciation as the model form, from which the speech of the rest of us 'varies'. In contemporary debates, and indeed Ofsted policy, an old myth is doing the rounds again: that teaching 'standard English' speech will produce social mobility. To which claim, it might reasonably be asked: with regard to what other type of prejudice (because, at root, the standard language ideology informs a whole set of prejudices against particular speakers) are those who are discriminated against asked to mimic those who are doing the discriminating?

'Us' is complex in another way too. Historically, 'us' has functioned grammatically as the objective case of the pronoun 'we' – as the direct object of a verb ('God save us'), the indirect object of a verb ('she sent us some money'), or the object of a preposition ('she's one of us'). In each of these cases, evidently, the word signals plurality. Yet in Liverpool (and indeed in other places such as Dublin and Newcastle), 'us' can be used grammatically to refer to a single person in exactly the same way: 'ler us have hould of the basket' (Shimmin 1863: 6); 'here, give us one and I'll take it to him' (Owen 1961: 81); 'puts her arms around us and slides her hand down me trackies' (Sampson 2001: 217). In these examples, 'us' functions in the same way as 'me' (the objective case of the first-person pronoun 'I'). Now this raises the issue of the categorization of the language of Liverpool, specifically in relation to 'Standard English'. In fact, the *OED* records the use of 'us' in the singular mode as 'chiefly in unemphatic use (frequently with *give*): me; to me', and glosses it as '*English regional, Scottish, Irish English*, and *colloquial*'. But again this raises more questions than it answers. If 'us' is 'English regional' – say Liverpudlian – then is it grammatically correct for a speaker of Liverpool English to use this form? Does it matter if they are 'educated'? If it is grammatically correct, then how does that square with the fact that 'Standard', with reference to 'language', is defined by the *OED* in the current edition as a term 'applied to that variety of a spoken or written language of a country or other linguistic area which is generally considered the most correct and acceptable form'. Hmmm. Is 'us' both correct and incorrect? Correct if a Liverpudlian is speaking Liverpool English but incorrect if they are trying to use Standard English? Is 'us' correct when speaking 'colloquially' but not otherwise? But what does 'colloquial' mean? The *OED* gives: 'belonging to common speech; characteristic of or proper to ordinary conversation, as distinguished from formal or elevated language'. So, if a Liverpudlian is using the 'common speech' of her city, as opposed to the 'formal or elevated language' of Standard English, 'us' is correct? But not otherwise? The truth is that this nonsensical farrago of categories is a form of prescriptivism in the guise of what linguists self-flatteringly call descriptivism (they do this in order to set themselves up as 'objective scientists'). It is prompted by an often unwitting desire, historically deeply rooted and quite general in British culture, to fix forms of speech in a hierarchy that privileges the language of some and downgrades the language of others ('non-standard' very quickly becomes 'sub-standard', as I indicated in the Introduction). Categories matter in that they help us to make sense of the world ('Liverpool English' is a category, as is 'Scouse'!) But linguistic categories are historically constructed modes of classification and, as such, they embody all sorts of specific social interests. It can happen – and often does – that our categorical ways of thinking about language blind us to such factors.

'Us' isn't the only term in Liverpool English that raises these issues. 'Youse', for example, is the plural of 'you' (recorded from the early twentieth century: 'Now, ladies, if youse will get out of the cab' (Hanley 2009 [1936]: 392). Probably imported from Irish English, in which they are retained, the forms 'youse'/'yous'/'yez'/'yiz' are also used in the United States, Canada, Australia, New Zealand, South Africa and, indeed, in areas of Britain other than Liverpool. From a historical perspective, the 'you' (singular)/'youse' (plural) forms constitute a reformulation of a distinction that used to be marked in English by 'thou'/'thee' (singular) and 'ye'/'you' (plural) (with the added feature that 'thou'/'thee' signalled familiarity and 'ye'/'you' denoted some form of social respect – a characteristic known in linguistics as the 'T-V' distinction, from Latin *tu* and *vos*. George Fox, the seventeenth-century English Dissenter and founder of the Quakers, felt strongly enough about the thou/ye singular/plural distinction to write a very long book about it – *A Battle-Door for Teachers & Professors to Learn Singular & Plural You to Many, and Thou to One* (1660). At the time, however, there were consequences for using what Fox considered to be the correct grammatical forms ('thou'/'thee'), rather than the forms that signalled social superiority ('ye'/'you'), as he notes in *A Journal*:

> For Thou and Thee was a sore cut to proud flesh, and them that sought self-honour; who, though they would say it to God and Christ, would not endure to have it said to themselves. So that we were often beat and abused, and sometimes in danger of our lives for using those words to some proud men, who would say, 'What! you ill-bred clown, do you Thou me!' (Fox 1694: 245)

Given that the singular/plural distinction is useful and widely used in forms of English, is Liverpool English 'youse' non-standard? If it is, is it correct? Is it in fact a better (because more accurate) use of language? If not, why not? Another example is 'hisself', a much-stigmatized form of 'himself' (the *OED* gives it as 'regional and colloquial' again), as in Niall Griffiths's Liverpool English novel *Kelly and Victor* (2002): 'for some soft-arsed fuckin reason known only to hisself' (Griffiths 2002: 44). But, as well as featuring in contemporary use, 'hisself' is also a historically attested form, recorded in the *OED* from the fourteenth century, as for example in the anonymous *Meditations on the Life of Christ* (1450): 'mekely he clothys hys selfe as he hade bene þe lawest' ('humbly he clothed his self as if he were the lowest'). In Griffiths's case, 'hisself' is evidently used as a stylistic aspect of characterization, but the real question is why this feature is available for this purpose. Given that it is a historically attested form, and that it is used in contemporary Liverpool English, why can it be used to represent (as it is in Griffiths's novel), not simply the fact that the character comes from Liverpool, but also social characteristics such as class and scallywaggery (with associations of anti-social behaviour)? Similar questions can be posed about the use of forms such as the double negative and the past tenses of various verbs: 'clumb' ('I clumb over the wall'); 'come' ('I come straightaway'); 'drug' ('the scuffers drug him out'); 'took' ('it was took'); 'them' ('them two were a pair'); 'was' ('I wish you was'). Stylisticians are quick to identify such features and their associated social features in literary texts; they're not quite as adept at analysing the hierarchical ordering of language that underpins this practice.

Tony Harrison's 'Them and [Uz]' was published in 1978, the year I went to university; I wish I'd read it then. It is a meditation not just on the pronunciation of 'us', but on the ways in which the stratified, hierarchical, power-laden nature of language in Britain relates to questions of class, education and culture. It features the voice of a teacher addressing a working-class pupil by invoking the prose/poetry distinction: 'Poetry's the speech of kings. You're one of those/Shakespeare gives the comic bits to: prose!'. But the crucial difference lies at the level of pronunciation: 'All poetry (even Cockney Keats?) you see/'s been dubbed by [ʌs] into RP' (Harrison 2016: 133).

I was given one of the comic roles too: Hortensio in *The Taming of the Shrew* in the 1977 co-production mounted by Sneddies and Bellerive, a Catholic girls' grammar school (motto: 'Suaviter in Modo Fortiter in Re' – 'Gentle in manner resolute in execution'; aye, if you like). In the play, Hortensio woos Bianca and, to pursue his suit, he pretends to be a music teacher; having none of it, she smashes a lute over his head. Cue the entrance of *'Hortensio with his head broke'*: 'And with that word she struck me on the head,/And through the instrument my pate made way' (II i 153–5). All very funny and all, but the director thought it might add to the amusement if I pronounced 'pate' as 'pâté', which would have been a class-based joke mocking my ignorance (I'd never heard of *pâté*, a French word that you could translate as 'paste' or 'pastry'). Suavely I swerved that and resolutely stuck on the night to 'pate'; who am I to mess with the bard?

Towards the end of 'Them and [Uz]', the poetic persona marks a transition in his own attitude:

I chewed up Littererchewer and spat the bones
into the lap of dozing Daniel Jones,
dropped the initials I'd been harried as
and used my name and own voice: [uz] [uz] [uz].
(Harrison 2016: 133)

I read English littererchewer and langwidge as my degree too, and Daniel Jones the phonetician featured in my doctoral research on 'Standard English' (in his *Outline of English*

Phonetics – the standard textbook for a long period – Jones chose 'as the standard of English pronunciation the form which appears to be most generally used by Southern English persons who have been educated at the great English public schools': Jones 1922: 4). The particular form of my education impeded *and* liberated me and, like Harrison, it took a while before I found my voice and worked out what I wanted to say. There is a difference though, since 'Them and [Uz]' declares a return to 'the language that I spoke at home'. It wasn't like that for me. I never did stop speaking my version of the language of home: I say /ʊs/ or /ʊz / because I can't say anything else. If the Royals have their 'we', then /ʊs/ and /ʊz / belong to us.

VAULTS

'The vaults' was a term that older speakers used instead of the now standard 'pub'; it featured, for example, in the name of my dad's local, 'The Wellington Vaults' ('The Wellie') on Mill Street in the Dingle. Originally an architectural term, 'vault' developed to refer to an enclosed space with an arched roof, particularly a basement area, and then later to mean a cellar area of this kind used to store goods or, specifically, booze. Hence in Thomas Nashe's 'Summer's Last Will and Testament' (1592), Summer (Sir Robert Tosspot) denounces Bacchus (the god of wine) and his 'swynish damn'd-borne drunkennes': 'Bacchus for thou abusest so earth's fruits/ Impris'ned live in in cellars and in vawtes' (Nashe 1883: VI 134).

Drinking used to be strictly regulated in Britain, a legacy of DORA – the Defence of the Realm Act (1914). Pubs were closed in the afternoons, from 3.00–6.30 (2.30–7 on Sundays), and time was called at 10.30 weekdays (10 on Sundays). 'Have yez no homes to go to?' landladies shouted; 'You wouldn't be shouting that if you had to go to our house', was the standard reply. The rules were finally loosened in 1988 (11–11 drinking was allowed) and then 2003 (New Labour's 24-hour rule). Before that, if you wanted to drink outside those tight hours, you had two choices: you bought 'fender ale' for home consumption from the 'offy' ('off-licence sales'). Or you had to find a pub that offered (in some places it seemed compulsory) a 'lock-in'. There were plenty of locals that provided this generous social service, which was usually accessed by an ostentatiously surreptitious after-hours knock on the window. 'The Wellie' had a sign on the bar that read: 'Happy Hour 11–2'; it didn't specify whether the 11 in question was am or pm.

Drinking was part of the initiation into the masculine adult world and there were various rituals and semiotic codes that you had to learn. Some were linguistic – the names for drinks for example, which were graded in terms of preference. From 'bitter', to a named brand, to sophisticated mixed drinks such as 'brown bitter (half of bitter, half of bottled brown ale); 'brown mild', also known as a 'boilermaker' (half of mild, half of bottled brown ale); 'fifty' (half of mild, half of draught Guinness); 'golden' (half of bitter, half of lager); and so on. Knowing the names of pubs mattered too, or at least knowing the names by which pubs were known. Some were relatively easy: 'The Wellie' (as above), 'The Eastern' ('The Great Eastern'), 'The Poet's' ('The Poet's Corner') 'The Farmer's' ('The Farmer's Arms'), 'The Volly' ('The Volunteer Arms' – the last pub on Park Road before town). Others were more mysterious: 'Blacks' or 'Black George's' ('The Royal George'), 'The Dead House' ('The Derby Arms'), 'Dirty Dick's' ('The Mersey View'), 'Jessie Appleton's' ('The Dingle'), 'Knob Hill' ('The High Park'), 'Heartbreak Hotel' ('The Queen's Head'), 'Peg Legs' ('The Herculaneum Bridge'), 'The Sixie' ('The Mount'). Other rituals were behavioural and included whether you stood at the bar or sat at a table, whether you went in the bar or the snug (both practices were gendered), and how you dressed. My father and his friends regularly wore jackets and ties (if not suits) to the pub, and being 'sharp' was a matter of pride (as noted previously, in this respect, at least, I was a source of constant if wistful disappointment to my father). Buying a 'round' (a seventeenth-century coinage) was, of course, the most important ritual of all. In fact, standing 'rounds' had been outlawed as part of the anti-alcohol legislation in the

First World War– the 'Anti-Treating Order'. But 'mugging' someone, which meant buying them a drink (a 'mug'), rather than robbing a stranger in the street (from 'mug', 'ugly face'), was an important social practice in Liverpool and reneging on it was a serious social offence. Some people, who'd had enough, bought a round as they were leaving the pub to ensure their good communal standing.

Women were not expected to go to the bar, and if they drank beer it was served in a 'lady's glass' (a half pint). Working-class feminism (though that's not what it was called) put an end to that in the 1980s, though it provoked absolute consternation among older men when their daughters started insisting on pints. Some men bought two halves – therefore conforming to their rule about 'ladies' glasses' – rather than buy a woman a pint. The young women were hardly constrained though, as they gaggled in a mobile show of extravagant fashion (they dressed for each other), heading determinedly from pub to pub towards the ultimate destination: 'town'. Flirtatious, funny and loud, brazening out the social wreckage wrought by Thatcherism, at least for the night, they weren't to be messed with. God help the man (because he was beyond earthly power) who thought he could intrude on their hard-defended, intimate, boozy, solidarity. It was always worth watching when it happened though (schadenfreude and all that – from the German *schaden*, 'harm', and *freude*, 'joy'), and more than once I saw a landlady intervene to rescue a male mishap who fancied his chances. 'Alright, girls, alright, you've had your fun', she'd say; but they hadn't – they were usually just starting for the night. It was carnival – full of mockery, disruptive laughter, exaggeration – the world turned upside down. And the next day it was back to reality (I almost wrote 'back to work', but there was little if any work in working-class Liverpool in the unemployed 1980s).

Pubs were part of a way of life – localized, intense and long-established. On nights out you wandered peripatetically from smoke-filled pub to smoke-filled pub ('you can't stop, you'll take root'); they were centres of stories, laughter, music and song. One regular in 'The Wellie' could recite that well-known American (well, Canadian) import, 'The Shooting of Dan McGrew', in its entirety – from 'A bunch of the boys were whooping it up in the Malamute saloon' to the revelation, fifty seven lines later, that 'The woman that kissed him and – pinched his poke – was the lady that's known as Lou'; it was a mnemonic feat. Pubs were also the place for arguments – about anything and everything – and political disputes. There was always one working-class Tory, though they always defended themselves spuriously with 'I'm not saying I'd vote for her'. Drink and politics were also part of the Oxford scene later, though I was surprised to find that alcohol was cheaper in the Lindsay bar at Balliol than 'The Wellie', and in my own college the bar ran on an honesty book system (with predictable results). It was an early lesson in the ways in which the middle class subsidizes itself. Oddly enough, though students in the bar may have been short of money, none of them faced chronic poverty, but more than a few of them seemed remarkably unfamiliar with the practice of buying a round. 'The Wellie', on the other hand, for better or worse, was full of poor people fighting to be generous, struggling to maintain values that rose above the dominant message of crude individualism. As a student in the Dingle, it was hard to buy a drink; 'put your money away, lad', 'his money's no good', 'don't insult me', 'you can buy me one when you're earning' ... The plethora of pubs on Mill Street and Park Road have gone now – from twenty or thirty there may be a couple left – along with the banks and churches. The pubs were casualties of the deregulation and low taxation of alcohol; their disappearance marks the passing of a particular form of working-class culture.

The language of drinking is as historical as any other form of language. My dad knew the names of measures of drink that had disappeared by the time I was accompanying him to 'The Wellie'. A 'pony', recorded from the eighteenth century though its etymology is unknown, was a small glass of beer – about a quarter of a pint (the term also meant – usually to gamblers – £25). In addition, a 'dodger' or 'Peter Hudson' referred to about a third of a pint. The etymology is obscure in both cases, though, probably apocryphally, 'Peter Hudson' is claimed to be the name of a Liverpool brewer who limited his morning intake to the specified amount. The real innovations in alcohol-related vocabulary, however, lay in the coinage of terms meaning 'drunk'. They included 'arseholed' (an abbreviation of 'pissed as arseholes', though the derivation of that phrase is unclear); 'bevvied' (from 'beverage', recorded from the late nineteenth century); 'bladdered' (from the late twentieth century, presumably from a full bladder); 'boxed' (an Americanism, from nineteenth-century 'box', 'head'); 'half seas over' (a nautical legacy – originally meaning 'half way across the sea', first recorded in Liverpool Municipal Records in 1551); 'hammered' (a late twentieth-century extension of 'hammered', 'beaten out of shape with a hammer' – self-inflicted damage); 'kaylied' (an early twentieth-century adaptation of the Irish céilidh, 'social evening, party'); 'legless' (a nineteenth-century Americanism – too drunk to stand); 'lush' or 'lushed' (from the eighteenth-century cant term 'lush', 'liquor, drink'); 'mopsed' (from an eighteenth-century use of 'mop' meaning 'to drink' or 'drink up'); 'muzzied' (from the eighteenth-century 'muzzy', 'confused, vague'); 'one over the eight' (early twentieth-century Forces' usage, apparently from the belief that up to eight drinks was a safe amount); 'parlatic' (a late nineteenth-century borrowing from Irish English, a corruption of 'paralytic', 'paralysed'); 'pissed' (recorded from the early nineteenth century, presumably related to 'bladdered'); 'plastered' (an early twentieth-century coinage – 'Get plastered, you bastard, Happy Birthday to you ...'

– derivation unclear); 'raddled' (recorded in English from the seventeenth century, probably by association with 'addled', 'confused'); 'scoused' (from the early twentieth century, origin unknown, though possibly a combination of 'souse' – 'pickled', hence very drunk – and 'scouse'); 'stewed' (an eighteenth-century Americanism – 'soaked in liquid'); 'well away' (a mid nineteenth-century abbreviation of 'well on the way to getting drunk'); 'wellied' (not from staying in 'The Wellie' too long, though there was always that danger, but possibly from either 'well away', or, more likely, 'to welly', 'to kick hard' – presumably with wellies on); 'wrecked' (an Americanism – an extension of 'wrecked', 'very damaged, destroyed'). An ABC of self-harm. Of course, those who went too far were met with the dreaded words 'tap stopped', which meant that you were barred until further notice. It was not a judgment that was open to argument.

'Booze' was the common word for alcohol, and it gave rise to 'boozer', meaning both pub and someone who drank heavily, if not excessively, a sense that gives a link to its etymological origins. The derivation is from early modern Dutch *buizen*, 'to drink to excess', probably from Middle High German *bûs*, 'blown-up condition, tumidity' (or, as we now say, 'beer-belly'). The first use in English is in a fourteenth-century satire on Irish monks;

Hail ȝe holi monkes wiþ ȝur corrin
late and raþe iffilid of ale and wine
depe cun ȝe bouse þat is al ȝe care.
(Furnivall 1862: 154)

(Hail ye holy monks with your drinking pots
filled early and late with ale and wine
heavy drinking is all you care about.)
(My translation)

You didn't have to be a 'misery moo' (a miserable teetotaller who drank milk) or a temperance evangelist from the 'Sally

Gash' (Salvation Army) to know that boozing – in the sense of drinking to excess – was a problem. Often enough, the generosity of pub behaviour required spending money that properly belonged elsewhere, and the givers and beneficiaries were usually men looking after other men. Getting 'rotten', a late nineteenth-century Australian coinage meaning 'very drunk', often necessarily entailed behaviour that was 'rotten' ('base, corrupt', a fourteenth-century extension of the original meaning of 'decomposing flesh'). There were too many homes that paid the price for the money spent in what were, apart from those carnivalesque moments mentioned earlier, and the labour of the women who worked behind the bar, predominantly male houses.

Oxford floated on alcohol too, though the costs were different in every sense. One locale that I frequented was the Bullingdon Arms on Cowley Road; it was a meeting place for the town's Irish community and it hosted good quality *ceol agus craic* (music and craic). There was, however, another Bullingdon, a notorious private members club whose all-male clientele was restricted to members of the ruling class; its speciality was drunken sessions in which restaurants were wrecked. After such events, the damages were paid for and quietly forgotten. Now just imagine if a group of working-class Liverpool lads wrecked a restaurant but went back the next day and paid for it. 'And the case for the defence, your honour, is that these young men, under the influence of alcohol, behaved badly but made immediate restoration and ask simply that all be forgotten …'. They wouldn't get the time of day. Rotten indeed.

WOOLLYBACK

Perhaps the Liverpudlian's greatest fear is to be taken for a woollyback, since in Liverpool parlance it's a terrible accusation to have levelled at you. Of course, if you're from certain parts of the city, it could never be applied to you – except in some horrible metaphorical jest. But if you live out towards the borders, it's always there lurking – the possibility that you might be taken to be a 'woollyback', 'woolly' or indeed just a 'wool' (the plazzymorph 'wool' is the most common form of the term today). And if you're from St Helens, or Widnes, or the Wirral, or, well, any number of other places beyond core Liverpooldom, then it's just inevitable that the epithet will follow you round to the end of your days.

The derivation of 'woollyback' is complicated. 'Woolly' was a late nineteenth-century Americanism meaning 'country person', with an implicit reference to farmers and sheep (the related term 'sheepshagger' makes the link evident, with the important distinction that being a 'woollyback' can't land you in jail in and of itself, whereas being a sheepshagger might). In this sense the term is an example of an old hierarchy that saw city life as 'civilized' (from the Latin *cīvĭtas*, 'city') and rural life as backward and unsophisticated. But in Liverpool English 'woollyback' had a very specific usage: in the Liverpool police force from the 1960s it referred pejoratively to uniformed officers – because the uniforms were made of wool – and/or to officers not working within the city boundaries (presumably because of the earlier association between 'woolly' and the countryside). From that origin, the term extended to become a general term of abuse, at first referring to people from just outside Liverpool – particularly Lancashire, Cheshire, or North Wales – who aren't conversant with the ways of the big city. Later, the meaning extended further to mean just anyone who isn't from Liverpool and thus ignorant of its supposedly superior ways.

Evidently this Liverpudlian self-regard is part of the city's identity formation, and it has specific historical roots. One element of this process is the long-standing rivalry between Liverpool and Manchester, as exemplified in the nineteenth-century distinction between 'Manchester men and Liverpool gentlemen'. Though it should be remembered that what appears like a class distinction here (based on the idea that in Manchester they made things, whereas in Liverpool they traded them), is in fact a distinction within the dominant class itself (factory owners versus mercantilists). The urban rivalry went deep and was expressed in economic, political and cultural terms, though it was hardly uni-directional. 'Dicky Sam', the most common nickname for Liverpudlians in the nineteenth century (within the city and beyond), originated in Lancastrian contempt for the port's big-wigs. Anachronistically, you might call it the 'woollyback's' revenge.

Given that language is one of the principal means by which we encounter and evaluate each other, the status of 'woollyback' is often mediated in terms of speech. Another way of putting it is that accent is a dead give-away. Again, there is evidence to suggest this is not a recent development. In the early nineteenth century, William Shepherd's satire, *The True and Wonderful History of Dick Liver* (1824), indicates that there was a marked distinction between Liverpool and its surrounding area in terms of language. In Shepherd's text, 'Dick Liver', a 'smooth-tongued' Dicky Sam, constantly outwits a Mancunian cotton spinner, Tom Twist (possibly the first 'woollyback'). Pointedly, Dick 'laughed at [Tom's]

Lancashire dialect', including utterances such as: 'Dom the sceawndrill, I'll be deigh'd if I e'er trust him agen' (Shepherd 1824: 7). The great Lancastrian linguistic divide was certainly clear by the late nineteenth century. James Picton, the famous Liverpool architect and historian, asserted that 'the cities of Liverpool and Manchester, only thirty miles apart, differ materially in their dialect' (Picton 1888: 210). And in a comment on Prime Minister Gladstone's accent (Gladstone was born on Rodney Street in the city centre and raised in Seaforth), Picton noted that Gladstone's 'tones and mode of utterance are decidedly of Liverpool origin. We bring our words out "ore rotundo," without the mincing word-clipping of the cockney and equally distant from the rough Tim Bobbin Lancashire dialect' (Picton 1888: 210). There is a lightly disguised sense of superiority in Picton's observation and he pinches 'ore rotundo' (literally 'rounded mouth') from Horace in the *Ars Poetica*: 'Grais ingenium, Grais dedit ore rotundo Musa loqui' ('To the Greeks the Muse gave ingenuity, to the Greeks it gave eloquent speech'). To Cockneys the Muse gave mincing clipped words, Mancs got a rough dialect, and Scousers were given the power to express themselves eloquently. As a contemporary Dicky Sam might say: 'nice one Musey'.

That isn't quite the typical evaluation of Liverpudlian speech, of course, either in the past or present. The first mention of 'Liverpudlian English' is in William Tirebuck's *Dorrie* (1891), in which one character passes judgment on the language of Dorrie, a working-class Liverpudlian, by saying that 'he didn't like the common Liverpool twang about her pronunciation' (Tirebuck 1891: 189). Dixon Scott, in a text that celebrated the 700th anniversary of the founding of Liverpool, commented on the North End, where the inhabitants 'speak a bastard brogue: a shambling, degenerate speech of slip-shod vowels and muddied consonants' (Scott 1907: 144). While in *City of Departures* (1946), by Liverpool novelist John Brophy, one character reflects: 'He had forgotten the ugliness of the Liverpool accent: his ears were not attuned to its adenoidal whine, its flat vowel sounds and slurred consonants, its monotonous rhythms compounded of distant memories of Dublin slums and Welsh villages, but all debased, forced through nasal and oral passages chronically afflicted with catarrh. Liverpool had the ugliest accent in the world' (Brophy 1946: 70).

Given that the distinctiveness of Liverpudlian speech had been noted in the early nineteenth century, it is significant that the stigmatization of Liverpool speech dates only from the very end of that century. In fact, contempt for working-class speech is more than a Liverpool affair and forms part of a sustained rejection of working-class culture in general that coincides with the 'threat' posed by universal suffrage and universal education – 'the rise of the masses' as it is sometimes condescendingly known. The confusion around 'Standard English' is a related example of it. Nevertheless, as outlined in the introduction, it is notable that, at least at the national level, the widespread contempt for Liverpool speech has continued to the present day.

But if language is a key medium that mediates between the Liverpudlian and the woollyback, the key question is: where does woollybackdom start? In other words, where is the linguistic boundary line? The evidence suggests that the border has changed historically. M.E. Francis's *Maime O' the Corner* (1898), set in Crosby (just north of Bootle, at the northern end of the city), is full of characters talking in what can only be a representation of Lancashire dialect: 'We haven't got no brass, yo' see, and hoo'd nobbut jest com out th'infirmary. I hadn't nought for her – no mate nor nought, an I bethought me as if yo' knowed, yo happen soom on yo' be good to her for the sake of owd times, an' when I'm in wark again I could pay for't' (Francis 1898: 296).

And my nan, born and bred under the bridge in Garston

(at the southern end of the city), spoke with an accent that contained several woollyback pronunciations – 'lurry' for 'lorry', 'tong' for 'tongue', for example. Later, slum demolition and 'urban redevelopment' confused the boundaries considerably. Widnes and St Helens are nearer to the Pier Head than the new towns of Runcorn and Skelmersdale respectively, but the latter are full of ex-pat Liverpudlians with impeccable Scouse accents that distinguish them from their woollyback neighbours.

Or, at least, that was the situation until relatively recently. Because the strange thing is that, despite being treated with disdain nationally, Liverpool English is now spreading into areas that were once indisputably woollyback. In addition to which, Liverpool English appears to be resisting the process of what linguists call 'dialect levelling' (by which certain features of a specific dialect are gradually replaced with features that have a wider provenance). This is probably explicable in terms of Liverpool's recent history. The disastrous decline of the city after the introduction of Thatcherite neoliberalism, and its reinvention as a heritage and tourism centre, both contributed to a developed insular identity – the sense of Liverpool as a place apart. In consequence, the linguistic aspect of the city's identity gained increased significance and, as one linguist has commented, in terms of specific features, 'Liverpool English is in fact getting *more* Scouse. Scouse is, we might say, getting Scouser' (Watson 2007: 237). But the spread of Liverpool English is more of a puzzle and it awaits detailed research. Why, to take just one example issue, would the younger generation in St Helens use features of Liverpool English (thus risking the taunt of 'plazzy Scousers'), whereas their parents use features belonging to Lancashire dialect? The answer has to be that some form of prestige influence is being exerted by Liverpool English, which is causing it to spread to areas such as St Helens, Widnes, and Wirral, at least for the younger generation. The fact that this counteracts the national trend is probably best explained by the fact that prestige operates on a number of different levels at the same time. In this case, it may be that features of Liverpool English are more attractive locally, as opposed to national features – linked to dialect levelling – that are associated with either 'the South' (a social abstraction as ridiculous as 'the North') or with 'posh'. If this is what's happening, I suppose we could call it Dicky Sam's revenge.

If language is no longer an accurate guide to woolly-backdom then, what are we to make of the category (after all, it isn't as though it's going away)? Perhaps it should be seen as what it always was – an insult that can be used to disparage non-Liverpudlians in a condescending way (Michael Owen was a Scouser until he left Liverpool and played for Manchester United, at which point he became a woollyback from Chester). It may be worth considering, though, whether the parochialism that underpins the insult does Liverpudlians and Mancs much credit. There are, after all, many more significant social battles to be fought than that between Dicky Sam and his woollyback neighbours.

XY

I don't know any Liverpool English words that begin with 'X', with the possible exception of 'the Xy', or, as it's also known, 'the Exxie', a plazzymorph for *The Liverpool Echo*. Now I could blag on about the history of that august publication, and indeed the history of newspaper publishing in Liverpool with its wide range of now defunct titles – *The Liverpool Courier, The Liverpool Daily Post, The Liverpool Evening Express* and *The Liverpool Mercury*. Or I could muse on the now lost term 'cosher', meaning newspaper lad (as recalled in James Callaghan's *Candles, Carts and Carbolic: A Liverpool Childhood Between the Wars*: 'Exy-cosher was our affectionate name for all paper lads': Callaghan 2011: 48). But sometimes, it's best to know when you're beaten by words, and 'X' has me stumped; time to ex-it.

YONKS

'Yonks' is one of those words that we used in school. I thought it had died out, but then the last time I was in St John's Market, I heard an older woman use it. I reflected (this is the sort of things linguists do while traipsing round town – it's an occupational hazard), that it must be generational, but then the next time I was at Anfield, one of my nephews used it. Who knows how words like 'yonks' get passed on and thus retained in the language? Is it through families? Age groups? Class? Gender? Race? Employment? Linguistic fashion? The truth is that we don't really know – it will probably be a complicated combination of a number of these factors and more. The answer to the question as to how words die, though, is much easier to answer: they fade from the language when people no longer have a use for them or when they are superseded by other terms. Our language is full of words that are now obsolete (if it weren't, the *OED* would be considerably smaller than the twenty volumes that constituted its last print edition), but 'yonks' isn't one of them. Where did it come from? There are a few accounts of its origins: one suggests that it is a sort of acronym – 'Y(ear)/mONth/weeKS' – while another claims that it may be a type of back slang involving 'donkeys' years'. A third suggests that it may be a Spoonerism (Dr Spooner was an Oxford don famous for accidentally transposing the initial sounds of words in a phrase – a type of metathesis – 'shining wit', for example). Thus 'donkeys' years' became 'yonkeys' dears' and thereafter, by shortening, 'yonks'. The truth is … we have no idea. And the same can be said for another phrase meaning a long time ago – 'when Donnelly docked' (who was Donnelly and when did he dock?); the antonym – 'when Nelson gets his eye back', meaning a long time in the future – is easier to decode.

There are plenty of other examples of words or phrases (or specific meanings) whose origins can't be explained precisely in Liverpool English past and present (though it's possible to guess at a some of them). Examples include (the ones with an asterisk were previously unrecorded before their appearance in *The Liverpool English Dictionary*): 'abnab'* (sandwich); 'the Aintree Iron'* (reference unknown, but The Scaffold told us we should be grateful for it); 'Ardy Alligan'* (old timer); 'bap'* (empty); 'barney' (fight, argument); 'Basil'* (fat man; policeman); 'bifter' (cigarette; joint); 'Black Maria' (police van); 'bog-eyed' (bleary-eyed); 'bogey'* (type of ollie); 'bonce' (head); 'box off'* (look after, take care of; complete); 'brassed off' (annoyed, fed up); 'bubble'* (to inform on); 'bun-oven'* (top hat); 'cabbaging'* (stealing); 'cady'/'caidy' (hat or cap); 'Cassoona'* (figure of mischief); 'chatty' (lousy); 'ching'* (five pounds); 'climp'* (very good, excellent); 'clobber' (clothes; general term for things); 'clock' (the face); 'to clock' (to hit someone, usually in the face; to notice someone, stare); 'to have a hard clock'* (to be cheeky, by analogy with 'hard faced'); 'clod' (a penny); 'clout' (blow, hard smack); 'to clout' (to hit); 'cod' (fool; nonsense); 'to cod on' (to acknowledge; pretend); 'cogger'/'coggy'* (Catholic); 'cooey'* (back alley, any out of the way corner or place); 'cosher'* (newspaper lad); 'Daddy Bunchie'* (Liverpool bogeyman; dandelion); 'delly'* (type of button used in children's game of pitch and toss); 'Dick Tutt'* (mythical Liverpool character); 'div'/'divvy' (idiot, fool, general insult); 'dodger'* (a glass of beer containing about a third of a pint; an eight-sided threepenny bit); 'donkey's years' (a long time); 'dosh', 'dough' (money); 'eenog'* (back-alley); 'fallies'* (bananas); 'Father Bunloaf'* (Catholic priest); 'first wet'* (or 'first lick'/'first biscuits' – said to someone who has just had a haircut, accompanied by a smack to the head); 'fudge'* (a farthing); 'gaff' (first rate, excellent); 'gate'* (bicycle); 'gazumped'* (tired out); 'gink' (wrongdoer); 'glannie'* (type of ollie); 'golly'* (tag); 'goss-eyed'* (cross-eyed); 'gozzy'* (cross-eyed); 'griffin'/'griff' (news, warning, tip); 'growler' (a tin for food used by dockers; sex offender); 'haines!'* (shout of retreat); 'Hickey the Firebobby'* (fictional Liverpool character); 'to holy stone' (to scour the deck of a ship); 'jasper' (cockroach); 'jaxy'/'joxy' (female genitalia); 'jigs'* (children's game); 'kewin'* (winkle); 'lad' (male of any age; sometimes used to signal an occupation); 'Liverpool button' (a makeshift button or toggle used by sailors); 'Liverpool clamp-down/ wash'* (sailors' usage – washing the torso); 'Liverpool head' (a ship's ventilation device); 'Liverpool tailor' (itinerant worker); 'lobbo'* (state of confusion); 'lug'/'lughole' (ear); 'lush' (a drink; a drunk); 'meff'* (term of abuse); 'meg' (halfpenny); 'Micky Dripping'* (anyone; anonymous); 'mind your own hindrance/sufferance' (mind your own business); 'mizzle' (to run away, disappear); 'moke' (horse, donkey; often used as an insult); 'monkey' (£500); 'mooch' (to cadge, scrounge); 'mush' (an outsider); 'to noak' (to keep watch, lookout); 'nonk'* (large clay marble); 'og'* (halfpenny); 'oggen'* (sea); 'ossie'* (house); 'Paddy Kelly'* (dock policeman); 'Paddy Rileys'* (the dock police); 'Paddy wack'* (pea soup; poor meat); 'pickie'* (threepenny bit); 'Pig and Whistle'* (crew canteen or bar on ship; a Liverpool pub); 'pinky'* (type of ollie); 'pong' (strong unpleasant smell'); 'pony' (a quarter of a pint of beer; £25); 'potty' (crazy, mentally unbalanced); 'prig' (to steal); 'quick- sticks' (very quickly); 'redneck' (a Catholic); 'ring taw'* (game of marbles); 'rody' (streaky – as in bacon); 'savoury ducks'* (faggots, meatballs); 'sett' (large paving stones); 'shaddle'* (seesaw); 'shammy round the block'* (to chase); 'shandry' (light cart); 'shindig' (party, dance); 'side' (to tidy up, clear away, put in order); 'skank' (steal, rob); 'skedaddle' (to move quickly away; escape); 'skin the dog'* (to get someone to buy drink); 'skrike' (scream, shriek); 'sky-blue pink with a finny-addy border'* (the acme; perfection); 'slack' (cheap, small inferior coal); 'sledder'* (thief); 'snitch' (nose); 'snout' (tobacco; cigarette); 'soojy-moojy' (scrub paintwork – on a ship, but by extension, elsewhere); 'sough' (gutter); 'sponds'* (money); 'spreck up'* (ejaculate); 'squallies'* (rubbish, leftovers); 'tank' (money); 'tanner' (sixpence); 'tom off'* (to stack cargo neatly on a ship); 'tusheroon' (half a crown); 'twern'* (swivel of watch chain; watch); 'twig' (to drink); 'vinegar trip'* (wasted journey); 'welt'* (unauthorized time-off); 'yankee' (a complex horse-racing bet on four selections, consisting of eleven separate gambles: six doubles, four trebles and a fourfold accumulator); 'yen'* (male homosexual); 'yip'* (to inform); 'yocker' (to spit); 'yodel'* (to abuse); 'yonk'* (to draw).

Many of these terms were or are used outside Liverpool, of course, though some of them weren't and aren't. There were in fact many other previously unrecorded terms that made it into the *LED*: 'abbadabba' (nonsense; meaningless language); 'agony' (in the sense of 'difficulty'); 'to ale' (drink); 'alica' (vinegar); 'alley apples' (stones); 'Aussie white' (Australian white wine); 'aways' (away games); 'back up' (to arrange a fire, usually at night, so that it would burn slowly); 'bad breath' (fruit loaf); 'band of Hope Street' (Royal Liverpool Philharmonic Orchestra); 'bangeroo' (sausage); 'banner socket' (navel); 'battle taxi' (police jeep); 'bawley' (rag and bone collector); 'bayoes' (baths); 'bed mates' (fleas); 'bed-wetter' (early riser); 'beer for dogs' (plentiful supplies); 'bellows to mend' (out of breath); 'belt' (blow, beating; effort; sex); 'bevy ken' (pub); 'big ears' (nosey person); 'binnie' (binman); 'bits' (scraps of meat at a butcher; scraps of potato or batter at a chippy); 'black and tan' (mixed drink – stout and mild); 'blackheads' (car keys); 'blackie' (police van); 'blad' (newspaper); 'blind man'/'blinder'/'blindy' (an alcoholic); 'blind scouse' (scouse without the meat); 'blocker' (bowler hat); 'blocker man' (supervisor); 'blocks' (cheap coal); 'blowing for tugs' (out of breath); 'blue frightener' (debt collection letter); 'blue paper with a duck on it' (summons from Liverpool City Council); 'bobbing' (skiving); 'bommie' (bonfire); 'bombdie' (bombed-out place – from the Second World War – or just derelict building); 'booze-jerk'/'booze-jerker' (bartender); 'booze-moke' (dray horse); 'booze-mopper' (heavy drinker); 'boozery' (brewery); 'boozing with the bugs' (drinking at home); 'boxed' (placed in a coffin or buried); 'boxer' (coffin-maker, undertaker); 'boys' pen' (section of Anfield reserved for boys); 'bread and spit' (dry bread; bread with a lick of margarine); 'break eleven' (to get caught, found out); 'breaks' (broken biscuits); 'bronzy' (suntan); 'bucket' (toilet); 'bucks'/'buckos' (gangsters); 'bum droops' (short legs); 'bumstarver' (badly fitting jacket); 'burst' (pee); 'Cabbage Hall Yank' (wannabe American); 'can lad' (apprentice, junior employee); 'carnival ribbons' (toilet rolls); 'Carpenters' day' (July 12th); 'carrying out' (midday meal, dinner); 'casey' (football); 'cat'/'catlick' (Catholic); 'catch-on' (dupe, fool); 'cheque on the knocker' (credit note for a store – repayable with interest); 'cherrywobs'/'cherrybobs'/'cherrywogs'/'cherrywags' (cherry stones used to play marbles); 'chip-chopper' (woodchip seller – for fires); 'chocolate port' (port that offers cheap amusements for sailors); 'choss' (chaos); 'Churchyard luck' (bitter comment on child mortality); 'cloggie' (clog-wearer); 'clonkers' (wooden clogs or heavy hobnailed boots; clog-fighting); 'coat-puller' (a favourite; tell-tale); 'coats off' (ready to fight); 'cockwood' (waste wood); 'cod boss' (foreman); 'cod on' (to acknowledge); 'Cogger's Circus' (the Catholic Cathedral); 'cop on with' (to meet; become acquainted with; become involved with); 'corky' (cricket ball); 'Count of Monte Cristo' (showy or well-dressed man); 'courter' (inhabitant of the notorious courts); 'cow-head' (idiot, fool); 'cowie' (cowboy film); 'cozzy' (swimming costume); 'crack on' (to acknowledge; to pretend; to inform, tell on); 'craggy' (serious, grumpy); 'crown jewels' (head, rather than genitals); 'Cunard feet' (splay feet); 'Cunard Yank' (Liverpool seaman influenced by American culture); 'cushty'/'custy' (beautiful, excellent); 'the Cut' (Liverpool–Leeds canal); 'cutty'/'cuddy' (bargeman; type of smoker's pipe); 'cutty shark' (small fish); 'cuzzies' (HM Customs officers); 'day old chick' (new worker on the docks); 'debby' (waste ground); 'desert wellies' (sandals); 'dewybar' (£2); 'dhobi' (the washing); 'dickie-dyke' (toilet attendant); 'dicky-docker' (Rabbi); 'diddy-mise' (abbreviate); 'diddys' (headlice); 'dixie'/'keep dixie' (to keep watch, keep a lookout); 'docker'/'docker's' (unusually large in size); 'Dockers' umbrella' (Liverpool Overhead Railway); 'dockology'/'doxology' (the lore and language of Liverpool dockers); 'dog' (corned beef); 'dollypeg' (leg); 'donkeystone' (cleaning stone); 'doorstopper'/'doorstep'/'doorknocker' (large sandwich); 'douse'/'to keep douse' (a warning; to keep watch); 'douser'/'dowse'/'dowsey' (a lookout); 'down the banks'/'to give someone down the banks' (to remonstrate, tell off); 'drom' (house); 'dubs' (toilet); 'eat'/'get eaten' (to be beaten comprehensively); 'erny' (undertaker); 'exchange' (swop deal involving council houses); 'fades' (bruised or sub-standard fruit sold cheaply); 'Father Christmas' (reluctant male sexual partner); 'fender ale' (beer drunk at home); 'fid' (marlin spike); 'firebobby' (fire officer); 'fish and money' (extortionate lending); 'flappers' (ears); 'Fleming's up the steps' (Paddy's Market); 'flies' cemeteries' (Eccles cakes); 'flock' (bed); 'frisby' (lesbian); 'Frisby Dyke' (Liverpudlian); 'funeral sugar' (cube sugar); 'funeral suit' (best suit); 'galosherman' (lamplighter; street worker); 'gegs' (gear); 'George Wiser' (Protestant); 'get off at Edge Hill' (*coitus interruptus*); 'ghosting' (skiving work); 'go-along' (smack, blow); 'gobshakes' (chatterbox); 'gog' (Welsh person); 'gom' (police); 'gozzy' (condom); 'gump stew' (chicken broth); 'gussie' (hat); 'half-time' (any interval during an event); 'Ham and Egg Parade' (cafés and restaurants in New Brighton); 'handball' (arrange cargo by hand on the docks); 'handy' (early, in good time); 'hanging the latch' (outstaying your welcome); 'Happy Harry' (misery-guts); 'hard knock'/'hard skin' (tough person); 'hatches are off' (pub opening time); 'hot kecks for' (keen on); 'hurry up van' (police van); 'in bulk' (laughing or disabled, incapacitated); 'in the meg specs' (ignorant, uninformed); 'in tucks' (laughing); 'jam butty car' (police car); 'jangler' (piano); 'jars out' (off-licence sales of alcohol; party time); 'jigger' (back alley); 'jigger-jerker' (sex in a back alley); 'jigger-rabbit' (stray cat); 'jink' (bringer of bad luck); 'job and knock' (to get paid for a job, not the time it takes to complete it); 'jockey' (a small glass used to top up beer); 'Joe Gerks' (jail); 'Johnny's shirt houses' (back-to-back terraced house); 'jowl'/'do a jowl' (run away); 'jowler-yowler' (stray cat); 'Judas burning' (see **bommie**); 'jump Sunday' (very infrequently); 'kayley' (sing-song, party); 'kecks down' (humiliation); 'knacker' (naked); 'knee-bender' (religious person); 'knife and fork tea' (full evening meal); 'knuckle butty' (punch); 'lanny' (landing stage'); 'last' (inferior, poor, disappointing; sad, embarrassed; mean towards – when used with 'on'); 'laughing bags' (well off); 'lazzy' (elastic); 'leave on' (leave a deposit on); 'let on to' (acknowledge); 'lib-lab' (library); 'Liverpoolese', 'Liverpudlianese' (the language of Liverpool); Liverpudlianism (a word or phrase found in Liverpool); 'living jockey-bar'/'living over the brush'/'living tally' (co-habiting in common law marriage); 'longees' (long trousers); 'the Loot' (period of the Liverpool police strike 1919); 'lugger' (eavesdropper); 'maccyowler' (stray cat); 'maggie ann' (margarine); 'make up man' (supplementary member of a team); 'Martin Enries' (cheap suits or second-hand clothes); 'measure your length in the river' (commit suicide); 'Mersey Funnel' (Liverpool's Catholic

Cathedral); 'mickey snatcher' (pigeon trapper); 'minesweeper' (someone who steals unattended food or drink); 'mingee' (police officer); 'misery hole' (miserable person); 'misery moo' (teetotaller); 'mopsed' (drunk); 'mumtip' (warning); 'musker' (police officer); 'naller' (catch); 'nark' (state of irritation; an argument; as a verb, to argue); 'nobber' (favoured worker); 'nothing down for you' (no chance of success); 'nudger' (long sandwich); 'oller' (waste ground); 'ollies' (marbles; testicles); 'one-eyed city' (Birkenhead); 'ovies' (overtime); 'ozzy' (hospital); 'Paddy's Wigwam' (Liverpool's Catholic Cathedral); 'Paradise Found' (Liverpool One); 'paralyse' (beat, hurt); 'parkie' (park watchman); 'pea whack' (soup); 'pepper thrower' (Catholic); 'pieces' (left-over, scraggy meat); 'pisspot jerker' (steward on a ship); 'plainees' (detectives); 'every Preston Guild' (once in a long time); 'proey' (programme); 'Professor Messer' (know-all, interfering person); 'puckle' (pull a face); 'pudding picking' (living off immoral earnings); 'pulverize' (beat up severely); 'Queen Anne front Mary Ann back' (pretentious); 'queen of the washhouse' (gossip); 'queg' (gay); 'rat catchers' (Catholics); 'redner' (blush); 'red-raddle' (red-coloured stainer for steps and window sills); 'rope' (to stitch); 'saddy' (cruel); 'Sally Gash' (Salvation Army); 'salt dolly'/'salt fish' (dried and salted fish); 'sandgrounder' (person from Southport); 'sandstone' (to scrub the front step); 'sanny' (hygiene inspector); 'sap' (to make someone bleed); 'sass' (sarsaparilla); 'savager cane' (police baton, originally a signalling stick); 'Scaldie' (Liverpool–Leeds canal); 'scallops' (potato in batter); 'sconehead' (insult); 'scoused' (drunk); 'scouseology' (all things Scouse); 'segs on his arse' (lazy); 'sherper' (socially ambitious person); 'shit creek' (the Mersey); 'side' (pavement); 'skip' (to board transport); 'slobbergob' (insult); 'slummy' (loose change); 'sly' (pitiable, unfortunate); 'snadger' (sparrow); 'sniff the barmaid's apron' (drink moderately); 'snot gobbler' (insult); 'soft lad' (insult);

'spammie' (love bite); 'spec' (place to watch from); 'spew' (leave, reject); 'spud' (hole in a sock); 'squatter' (toilet); 'squidge' (look at, examine); 'squirrel dance' (foreplay); 'stepdash' (to clean front steps); 'sterry' (sterilized milk); 'stewbum' (drunkard); 'stewbum palace' (police lock-up); 'stick man' (dapper, finicky man); 'strag' (stray); 'straightener' (fight to resolve an issue; punishment); 'sunbeam' (pious person); 'swill' (wash); 'talk Blundellsands' (talk posh); 'tanner doctor' (second-rate medic); 'tanner megger' (cheap football); 'tanroagan' (scallop – not to be confused with 'scallop'; see above); 'tap stopped' (barred); 'tip-scabbler' (rubbish dump scavenger); 'topshiner' (top hat); 'towels on' (Time!); 'tramstopper' (large butty); 'twang' (to preach); 'under the arm/crotch' (unwell); 'wagon' (bed); 'wayo' (wait; hold on); 'Welsh letter' (defective condom); 'when Donnelly docked' (a long time ago); 'when Nelson gets his eye back' (a long time in the future); 'whicker' (suit); 'yard dog' (insult).

'Yonks', and all those other words whose origins can't be explained, together with the previously unrecorded words, are fascinating for two reasons. First, because they exemplify the sheer energy (from the Greek, ἐνέργεια, enérgeia, 'practical activity') and creativity of the Liverpool vernacular. Second, because they illustrate the limits of our historical knowledge about language. And, as anyone who works in the history of our common language should acknowledge, we run up against those boundaries pretty quickly. Mind you, that doesn't stop people inventing all sorts of ingenious nonsense to fill in the gaps; it's part of the fun of the game – as long as it doesn't get mistaken for historical fact.

Z-CARS

One of the more amusing, and indeed gratifying, aspects of teaching at a university is that you get to meet students' parents at graduation, to their children's great embarrassment. This often entails profuse thanks on the part of the older generation for putting up with their offspring, and, sometimes, it is the occasion of surprising revelations. Grannies whose imminent death was the reason a student couldn't meet a deadline, for example, have been known to appear, often in remarkably rude health; a few have even returned from the dead. But at one memorable graduation, who should I see walking towards me, hand outstretched, impeccable Belfast accent hailing me, but Sergeant Lynch from *Z-Cars*. As I told him at the time, he was a very familiar figure from my childhood, as he rose from humble PC to the role of Inspector. It turned into a very pleasant afternoon with James Ellis the actor, whom, I am afraid to say, I called 'Bert' more than once. Bert Lynch was one of a formidable, almost exclusively male, *Z-Cars* cast, including Inspector Barlow (Stratford Johns); DS Watt (Frank Windsor); PC Fancy Smith (Brian Blessed); PC Graham (Colin Welland); DC Elliott (John Thaw); and DI Bamber (Leonard Rossiter).

Z-Cars (the title was a fictional call-sign rather than a reference to the Ford Zephyr and Ford Zodiac cars that the Rozzers used) was set in Newtown (Kirkby), a spill-over settlement built from the 1950s to the 1970s after slum clearance in Liverpool. 'Kirkby' is an Old Norse name, composed of the elements *kirk*, 'church', and *byr*, 'farmstead' or 'village', and testifies to Viking occupation (like later inhabitants of Liverpool, the Vikings came via Dublin). But although 'Newtown' was set just north of Liverpool, the nature of its ex-pat population meant that *Z-Cars* reflected the social developments that were taking place in the city next door at a crucial moment in its history. The social realism of the series, which often portrayed violent confrontation between scuffers and villains, and represented the link between poverty and crime, set it apart from the crass depiction of the police as guardians of community morals that typified *Dixon of Dock Green* and the like. There were no homilies at the end of *Z-Cars*, though of course the 'bizzies' invariably won; it was fiction after all.

Liverpool itself was known in *Z-Cars* as 'Seaport', though this was not the first fictional name for the city. John Owen coined 'Westport' in *The Cotton Broker* (1921), while Winifred Duke used 'Salchester' in *Household Gods* (1939), and James Hanley called Liverpool 'Gelton' throughout his remarkable five-volume history of the Fury family (1935–58). In fact the literary representation of the city, particularly in novelistic form, has a long and much-neglected history, ranging from searing critiques of mercantile capitalism in the early nineteenth century, to Anglo-Welsh and social reform novels towards the end of that period, early feminist works in the twentieth century, Hanley's expressionist masterpieces, social realist texts in the 1950s, and the more recent Scouse texts from the 1970s. From my point of view, one of the most interesting aspects of this largely unread tradition is the depiction of Liverpool English, though in the early work, at least, language is disregarded. For example, in William Maginn's *John Manesty, The Liverpool Merchant* (1844), a family drama involving slave-trading set in Liverpool in 1760, there is a simple refusal to transcribe local speech: 'We know enough of the *lingua Lancastriensis* to render us scrupulous of attempting an imitation, which we are conscious would be a failure. It is a good, solid, dialective variation of the Anglo-Saxon, which should not be spoiled by the mimicry of an intruder ... In not more, but less vernacular English, we shall proceed to tell our tale' (Maginn 1844: i 136)

By contrast, Silas Hocking's *Her Benny* (1879) draws a clear distinction between the urban (Liverpudlian) speech of the protagonist Benny, and the non-city speech of a countryman:

Just then he heard a countryman inquiring the way to Lime Street station, of a man who stood near him.

'Here's a chance,' [Benny] thought; and stepping forward, he said, 'I'll show you the way, sir, if yer likes.'

'Dost thee know th' way thysel', lad?' inquired the man. (Hocking 1966: 143)

The main linguistic interest in *Her Benny*, however, centres on Benny's moral journey from violence, poverty and degradation (he is falsely accused of stealing), to his final status as an upright, Christian, hero, as confirmed by his mastery of the social codes of correctness, including language. "'And he has the bearing of a gentleman, too," remarked Miss Munroe. "I expected we were going to be highly amused at his behaviour and his dialect, and so on; but he really speaks quite correctly'" (Hocking 1966: 181).

This ridiculous concatenation of language and moral status was a durable trope. An observer of Bristol miners in 1794 reported that fifty years previously they were 'barbarous and savage' and 'their dialect was the roughest and rudest in the Nation'. Yet as a result of religion instruction and education, he notes, 'they are much civilized and improved in principles, morals and pronunciation' (cited in Barrell 1983: 138). Much the same nonsense underpins one of the findings in a survey reported in the *Daily Mail* in 2013, which I discussed in the Introduction. The survey found that 29 per cent of the people asked found the Liverpool accent to be 'untrustworthy' (Woollaston 2013). It is hard to know who are the most idiotic – those who ask the question whether an accent is untrustworthy, those who answer it, or those who put the response in their newspapers.

Across a wide range of Liverpool literature then – from William Tirebuck's *Dorrie*, to James Haigh's *Sir Galahad of the Slums* (1907), John Owen's *The Cotton Broker* (1921), James Hanley's *Fureys* quintet (1935–58), and Alexander Baird's *The Mickey Hunters* (1957) – there are relatively few attempts to represent Liverpool speech. Indeed, even at the very moment when Scouse was being discovered, H.J. Cross's *No Language But a Cry* (1951) relied on features that, with the exception of the use of the word 'moke' (Liverpool English for horse or donkey, and by extension an insult), were more familiar from established depictions of Cockney dialect:

'Nah then, clever,' began the biggest tough, 'nah then, wot about it?'... Stamp on me bleedin' fingers, would yer?'...

'I ain't 'andin' over nothink'...

'Wot's the trouble, Mick? These mokes pickin' on you? (Cross 1951: 8–9)

The turning point in literary representations of Liverpool speech is perhaps predictably, but for obvious reasons, found in drama. Frank Shaw's *The Scab* (1952) was an important landmark in this respect and it begins:

Polly: Ere y'are, Jud, you may as well have summit. Want a bit of bread? *He shakes his head.* Nowt else. If dis ole strike goes on I spose we won't even ave de tea.

Jud: Aye, it's a terrible thing. *He takes tea from saucer.*

Polly: Ow many times ave I eard Barny say there never wud be a general strike?

(Shaw 1952: n.p.).

But the first serious, sustained, and successful attempt to depict the speech of Liverpool was found in the work of the Liverpool Welsh playwright Alun Owen: *No Trains to Lime Street* (1959), *After the Funeral* (1961), and *Lena, Oh my Lena* (1960) (all of which were TV dramas). The opening of *No Trains to Lime Street*, a drama of 'three sailors searching for themselves', is typical:

> CASS. Isn't it marvellous, eh! She's like a wink from a fancy woman! Liverpool ... the Garden of Eden of the North ... (*looking at his watch*) Eh up ... musn't keep you waiting love (*He blows a kiss out to the city*) ...
>
> BILLY (*almost dressed, opening the door*). Oh, for God's sake, Cass – you're like a big, soft kid! ... Some people have to work, like, for their living, y'know! ...
>
> CASS. Anyroad, forget your work, Billy, we're home! (Owen 1961: 15).

Owen's use of Liverpool accents and vernacular terms in this play was met with considerable criticism, against which he defended himself confidently:

> I have fought for two years now to get plays performed in the Liverpool accent. I've had a battle to get a love scene played in the dialect. I was told the accent was ridiculous, comical, absurd and very ugly. But I believe it is a very lovely accent. People get married, live and die using the Liverpool accent, so I see no reason why they should not make love in the Liverpool accent. I could quite easily have set this play in some never-never land of the north with everybody talking like Grace Fields. (Coles 1993: 203)

In literary terms, this confidence in the Liverpool vernacular carried over to its use in Alan Bleasdale's 'Scully novels' (based on radio dramas): *Scully* (1977) and *Scully and Mooey* (1984). These texts prepared the ground for the recent appearance of a number of 'Scouse' novels, including Kevin Sampson's

Awaydays (1999), *Outlaws* (2001), *Clubland* (2002) and *The Killing Pool* (2013); Niall Griffiths's *Kelly + Victor* (2002), *Stump* (2003) and *Wreckage* (2005); and Helen Walsh's *Brass* (2004). These 'Scouse' texts constitute a significant innovation in that they are written entirely in the vernacular, as in Griffiths's *Stump*:

> Yeh. Fuck me, am starving.
>
> Are yeh?
>
> Yeh. Pure fuckin Hank.
>
> We'll stop at a place just over the border well an get summin to eat. There's a postie a wanner check out anyway, see if it's screwable.
>
> Can't wait that long. I could eat a scabby head.
>
> Well, yill fuckin well have to fuckin wait. (Griffiths 2003: 13)

This confident and self-reflexive representation of the vernacular is a long way from the use of hackneyed literary conventions established in the nineteenth century to signal class and regionality. Which is not to say that this form of writing does not raise its own generic issues, not least with regard to the relationship between standard written English and the representation of speech. This is a complex area but, in short, the problem is this: if 'yill' in the line above is supposed to represent the speech of a Liverpudlian, then whose speech is represented by the standard written form 'you'll'?

Of course for most people familiarity with the representation of Liverpool speech has not been in written form at all. It has been mediated by a series of television dramas (and again the medium is significant) dating from the early 1960s to the recent past: from *Z-Cars*, through *Softly Softly*, *The Liver Birds*, *A Family at War*, *The Wackers*, *Boys from the Blackstuff, Bread, Merseybeat* and (for twenty-one years), *Brookside*. From police-station realism, to comedy based on the adventures of single women (a significant development), to a reflection of the role of the Second World War on middle-class family life in Liverpool, to stereotypical comedy of working-class manners, to the brutality of Thatcherism, and through to soap opera, the vernacular forms and accents of Liverpool have been presented, in varying degrees, to the British public. I suppose it's that tradition, at least in part, that we have to thank for those tedious moments when people who couldn't mimic a Liverpool accent to save their life, nonetheless greet a Liverpudlian with some stock phrase delivered in an excruciatingly painful misrepresentation of Liverpool speech.

Though he was from Belfast, James Ellis could do a good Liverpool accent (he had a role in *Boys from the Blackstuff*), but he had the good grace not to when we spent that afternoon discussing *Z-Cars*, Liverpool and Northern Ireland. He was a great fan of Brian Friel's *Translations* (a text I taught to his son) and he reminded me of a quote from the play: 'it is not the literal past, the "facts" of history, that shape us, but images of the past embodied in language' (Friel 1981: 66). I am sympathetic to this view, but in the end I am too much of a cultural and historical materialist to agree with it completely. It is the facts of history that shape us – the where and when of our social being – although evidently the images of the past (and present) embodied in language influence us too, not least because language is in and of itself a fact of history. Speaking, and thus sharing, a language is precisely, on an individual, subjective basis, to take part in, and to be shaped by, a social and historical form of life. Indeed my understanding of that principle underpins this book; it is what I have been attempting to convey in this series of brief accounts of words from Liverpool English, the language of the place from which I came and with which I continue to identify.

As I say, it was a very pleasant afternoon with Bert, and not a single granny rose from the dead to disturb us.

SELECT BIBLIOGRAPHY

Anon. 1821. 'D.S'. *The Kaleidoscope: or, Literary and Scientific Mirror.*

Baines, Edward. 1836. *History of the County Palatine and Duchy of Lancaster by Edward Baines ... The Biographical Department by W.R. Whatton.* London: Fisher, Son & Co.

Baird, Alexander. 1957. *The Mickey-Hunters.* London: Heinemann.

Barrell, John. 1983. *English Literature in History 1730–1780: An Equal Wide Survey.* London: Hutchinson.

Baxter, William. 1719. *Glossarium Antiquitatum Britannicarum, sive Syllabus Etymologicus Antiquitatum Veteris Britanniæ atque Iberniæ Temporibus Romanorum.* London: Bowyer.

B.E. 1699. *A New Dictionary of the Terms Ancient and Modern of the Canting Crew.* London: Hawes.

Belchem, John. 2006. *Liverpool 800: Culture, Character and History.* Liverpool: Liverpool University Press.

Bindloss, R.H. 1957. 'Why Scouser?'. *Liverpool Daily Post.* June 28th: 6.

Bowers, Fred. 2015 [1936]. *Rolling Stonemason: An Autobiography.* London: Merlin.

Brooke, Richard. 1853. *Liverpool as it was During the Last Quarter of the Eighteenth Century, 1775–1800.* Liverpool: Mawdsley.

Brophy, John. 1946. *City of Departures.* London: Collins.

Bryan, Tony. 2003. *99 Heyworth Street.* Liverpool: Bluecoat Press.

Burgess, Anthony. 2012. *Little Wilson and Big God.* London: Vintage.

Callaghan, James. 2011. *Candles, Carts and Carbolic: A Liverpool Childhood Between the Wars.* Lancaster: Palatine.

Camden, William. 1590. *Britannia siue Florentissimorum Regnorum, Angliae, Scotiae, Hiberniae, et insularum adiacentium ex intima antiquitate chorographica descriptio.* London.

Carlyle, Thomas. 1918 [1843]. *Past and Present.* New York: Scribners.

Channon, Howard. 1970. *Portrait of Liverpool.* London: Robert Hale.

Chaucer, Geoffrey. 1988. *The Riverside Chaucer.* 3rd ed. Oxford: Oxford University Press.

Clerk, Andie. 1971. *Arab. A Liverpool Street Kid Remembers: The Autobiography of an Early Century Street Arab.* Liverpool: self-published.

Coles, Gladys Mary. 1993. *Both Sides of the River: Merseyside in Poetry and Prose*. West Kirkby: Headland.

Cross, H.J. 1951. *No Language But a Cry*. London: John Murray.

Crowley, Tony. 2012. *Scouse: A Social and Cultural History*. Liverpool: Liverpool University Press.

Crowley, Tony. 2017. *The Liverpool English Dictionary*. Liverpool: Liverpool University Press.

'Daily Post' Reporter. 1955. 'A Proper Jangle in Scouser Lingo'. *Liverpool Daily Post*. July 1st: 6.

Defoe, Daniel. 2005 [1724–26]. *A Tour Through the Whole Island of Great Britain*. Ed. Pat Rogers. Harmondsworth: Penguin.

De Quincey, Thomas. 2000. 'Confessions of an Opium Eater' (1821, 1856). Vol. II. *The Works of Thomas De Quincey*. Ed. Barry Symonds et al., 21 vols., London: Pickering and Chatto.

Descriptive Catalogue of the Liverpool Museum of Anatomy. (n.d.). Liverpool: Matthews.

Dickens, Charles. 1985. *Oliver Twist*. London: Penguin.

Dibdin, Mr. 1781. 'Nautical Philosophy' in Anon, ed. *The Bull-Finch. Being a Choice Collection of the Newest and Most Favourite English Songs*. London: Robinson and Baldwin.

Dictionary of the Scots Language. 2004. http://www.dsl.ac.uk.

Duke, Winifred. 1939. *Household Gods*. London: Jarrolds.

Eden, Sir Frederic Morton. 1797. *The State of the Poor or, An History of the Labouring Classes in England, from the Conquest to the Present Period ... Together with Parochial Reports*. 3 vols. London: Davis.

Editorial comment. 1957. *Liverpool Daily Post*. June 27th: 6.

Ekwall, Eilart. 1922. *The Place-Names of Lancashire*. Manchester: Manchester University Press.

Elliott, Jim. 2006. *Once Upon a Time in Liverpool*. Bebington: Middleview.

Enfield, William. 1773. *An Essay Towards the History of Leverpool*. Warrington.

Farrell, John. 1950a. 'About that Liverpool Accent (or Dialect)'. *Liverpool Daily Post*. August 8th: 4.

Farrell, John. 1950b. 'A Guide to the Slang of Merseyside. This Half-Secret Tongue of Liverpool'. *Liverpool Daily Post*. August 25th: 4.

Fox, George. 1694. *A Journal or Historical Account of the Life, Travels, Sufferings, Christian Experiences and Labour of Love in the Work of the Ministry. Of that Ancient, Eminent and Faithful Servant of Jesus Christ, George Fox*. London: Northcott.

Francis, M.E. 1898. *Maime O' The Corner*. London: Harper and Brothers.

Fraser, Edward and John Gibbons. 1925. *Soldier and Sailor Words and Phrases*. London: Routledge.

Friel, Brian. 1981. *Translations*. London: Faber & Faber.

Furnivall, F.J. 1862. *Early English Poems and Lives of Saints*. Berlin: Philological Society.

Gower, John. 1901. *John Gower's English Works*. Ed. G. MacCaulay. Vol. II. London: Early English Text Society.

Griffith, R. 1950. 'Slang Words'. *Liverpool Echo*. December 14th: 6.

Griffiths, Niall. 2002. *Kelly + Victor*. London: Jonathan Cape.

Griffiths, Niall. 2003. *Stump*. London: Jonathan Cape.

Grose, Francis. 1787. *A Provincial Glossary, with a Collection of Local Proverbs, and Popular Superstitions*. London: Hooper.

Guardian. 1963. 'The Liverpool Sound'. October 8th: 9.

Halliwell, J.O. 1847. *A Dictionary of Archaic and Provincial Words, Obsolete Phrases, Proverbs and Ancient Customs, from the Fourteenth Century*. London: Smith.

Hanley, James. 1932. *Ebb and Flood*. London: Bodley Head.

Hanley, James. 2009 [1936]. *The Secret Journey*. London: Chatto & Windus.

Hanley, James. 2009 [1950]. *Winter Song*. London: Faber & Faber.

Harman, Thomas. 1567. *A Caveat for Commen Cursetors Vulgarely called Vagabones*. London: Gryffith.

Harrison, Henry. 1898. *The Place-Names of the Liverpool District; Or, The History and Meaning of the Local and River Names of South-West Lancashire and of Wirral*. London: Elliot Stock.

Harrison, Tony. 2016 [1978]. *Collected Poems*. London: Penguin.

Henri, Adrian, Roger McGough and Brian Patten. 1967. *The Mersey Sound*. Harmondsworth: Penguin.

Hignett, Sean. 1966. *A Picture to Hang on the Wall*. New York: Coward-McCann.

Hill, Judy. 1945. 'Let's Talk It Over'. *Liverpool Evening Express*. November 18th: 4.

Hocking, Silas. 1966 [1879]. *Her Benny*. Liverpool: Gallery Press.

Honeybone, Patrick. 2007. 'New Dialect Formation in Nineteenth-Century Liverpool: A Brief History of Scouse', in Grant, Anthony and Clive Grey. Eds. 2007. *The Mersey Sound: Liverpool's Language, People and Places*. Ormskirk: Open House Press.

Hotten, John Camden. 1860. *A Dictionary of Modern Slang, Cant, and Vulgar Words*. 2nd ed. London: printed by the author.

Isenberg, David. 1962. 'A Second Language – Standard English'. *Liverpool Echo*. July 9th: 6.

Jacques, J.B. 1973. *Get yer Wack*. Liverpool: Raven Books.

Jaques, J.B. 1975. *According to Jaques: A Mersey Bible*. Liverpool: Raven Books.

Jacques, J.B. 1977. *Scouse with the Lid Off*. Liverpool: Raven Books.

Johnson, Samuel. 1747. *The Plan of a Dictionary of the English Language*. London: Knapton.

Johnson, Samuel. 1755. *A Dictionary of the English Language; in which the words are deduced from their originals and illustrated in their different significations by examples from the best writers. To which are prefixed, a History of the Language, and an English Grammar.* London: Strahan.

Jones, Daniel. 1922. *Outline of English Phonetics.* Cambridge: Cambridge University Press.

Joyce, James. 1992 [1916]. *A Portrait of the Artist as a Young Man.* London: Penguin.

Lane, Linacre. 1966. *Lern Yerself Scouse, Vol. 2: The ABZ of Scouse.* Liverpool: Scouse Press.

Macklin, Charles. 1783. *The True-Born Irishman; Or, Irish Fine Lady.* Dublin.

Marson, Una. 2011. *Una Marson: Selected Poems.* London: Peepal Tree.

Marx, Karl. 1975. *Early Writings.* Harmondsworth: Penguin.

McClure, James. 1980. *Spike Island: Portrait of a British Police Division.* London: Macmillan.

Melville, Herman. 1849. *Redburn: His First Voyage.* New York: Harper & Bros.

Mistrolis. 1964. 'About Dem Scuffers'. *Liverpool Echo.* October 19th: 8.

Moloney, Peter. 1966. *A Plea for Mersey. Or, The Gentle Art of Insinuendo.* Liverpool: Gallery Press.

Nashe, Thomas. 1883. 'Haue with you to Saffron-Walden'. [1596]. In *The Complete Works of Thomas Nashe.* Vol. III. Ed. Alexander Grosart. London: printed for private circulation.

Nashe, Thomas. 1883. 'Summers Last Will and Testament'. [1592]. In *The Complete Works of Thomas Nashe.* Vol. VI. Ed. Alexander Grosart. London: printed for private circulation.

O'Hanri, Hari [an scríob]. 1950. 'It's The Irish In Us'. *Liverpool Echo.* December 13th: 2.

O'Mara, Pat. 1934. *The Autobiography of a Liverpool Irish Slummy.* London: Hopkinson.

Owen, Alun. 1961. *Three TV Plays: No Trams to Lime Street. After the Funeral Lena. Oh My Lena.* London: Jonathan Cape.

Owen, John. 1921. *The Cotton Broker.* London: Hodder and Stoughton.

Partridge, Eric. 1961. *A Dictionary of Slang and Unconventional English.* 2nd ed. New York: Macmillan.

Paulin, Tom. 1983. *Liberty Tree.* London: Faber & Faber.

Paulin, Tom. 1984. 'A New Look at the Language Question'. In *Ireland and the English Crisis.* Newcastle: Bloodaxe.

Picton, J.A. 1875. *Memorials of Liverpool: Historical and Topographical.* 2nd ed. rev. 2 vols. Liverpool: Walmsley.

Picton, J.A. 1888. 'Does Mr. Gladstone Speak with a Provincial Accent?' *Notes and Queries.* 7th Series. Vol. VI: 210–11.

'Postman'. 1942. 'Scouse and Scouser'. *Liverpool Daily Post*. August 1st: 2.

'Postman'. 1945. 'Jigger'. *Liverpool Daily Post*. December 11th: 6.

'Postman'. 1947a. 'Another Jigger'. *Liverpool Daily Post*. June 24th: 4.

'Postman'. 1947b. 'Jowlers'. *Liverpool Daily Post*. June 25th: 6.

Pratt, Mary Louise. 1991. 'Arts of the Contact Zone'. *Profession*. Modern Language Association: 33–40.

Puttenham, George. 1589. *The Arte of English Poesie*. London: Field.

Roberts, Eleazar. 1893. *Owen Rees: A Story of Welsh Life and Thought*. Liverpool: Foulkes.

Robinson, Peter. 1996. *Liverpool Accents: Seven Poets and a City*. Liverpool: Liverpool University Press.

Sampson, Kevin. 2001. *Outlaws*. London: Jonathan Cape.

Sayle, Alexei and David Stafford. 1989. *Alexei Sayle's Great Bus Journeys of the World*. London: Methuen.

Scott, Dixon. 1907. *Liverpool*. London: Black.

'"Scousers" Are All Brothers'. 1943. *Liverpool Evening Express*. December 4th: 2.

Shakespeare, William. 1974. *The Riverside Shakespeare*. Boston: Houghton Mifflin.

Shaw, Frank. 1950. 'Scouse Lingo – How It All Began'. *Liverpool Echo*. December 8th: 4.

Shaw, Frank. 1952. 'The Scab: A One Act Play set in Liverpool during the General Strike, 1926. With a Note on the Liverpool Way of Talking'. Typescript (author's personal copy). Liverpool Record Office.

Shaw, Frank. 1954. 'City of Nicknames'. *Liverpool Echo*. July 1st: 4.

Shaw, Frank. 1955. 'Death of a Dialect'. *Manchester Guardian*. April 20th, 18.

Shaw, Frank. 1957. 'Scouse Talks (text, with translations, of tape sound recordings made in Liverpool City Library)'. Liverpool Record Office.

Shaw, Frank. 1958. 'Dialect of a Seaport I'. *Journal of the Lancashire Dialect Society*. 8: 12–19.

Shaw, Frank. 1959a. 'Dialect of a Seaport II'. *Journal of the Lancashire Dialect Society*. 9: 32–41.

Shaw, Frank. 1959b. 'Strange Charm of the Lingo of Liverpool's Dockland'. *Liverpool Echo*. July 30th: 6.

Shaw, Frank. 1960a. 'Dialect of a Seaport III'. *Journal of the Lancashire Dialect Society*. 10: 30–42.

Shaw, Frank. 1960b. 'Ink, Lino and the Lenient Judge'. *Liverpool Echo*. June 20th, 5.

Shaw, Frank. 1966a. *Learn Yerself Scouse: How to Talk Proper in Liverpool*. Ed. Fritz Spiegl. Liverpool: Scouse Press.

Shaw, Frank. 1966b. 'Ollies in the Liverpool Olympics'. *Liverpool Daily Post*. August 8th: 4.

Shaw, Frank. 1971. *My Liverpool*. London: Wolfe.

Shaw, Frank and the Rev. Dick Williams. 1967. *The Gospels in Scouse*. Liverpool: Gear Press.

Shaw, George Bernard. 1916. *Pygmalion*. New York: Brentano.

Shepherd, William [Timothy Touchstone pseud.]. 1824. *The True and Wonderful History of Dick Liver*. Liverpool: Rushton and Melling.

Sheridan, Thomas. 1762. *A Course of Lectures on Elocution*. London: Strahan.

Shimmin, Hugh. 1863. *Liverpool Sketches*. Liverpool: Gilling.

Simpson, Matt. 1990. *An Elegy for the Galosherman*. Newcastle: Bloodaxe.

Skeat, W.W. 1896. 'Liverpool'. *Notes and Queries*. 8th series. Vol. IX: 173–4.

Spiegl, Fritz. 2000. *Scouse International: The Liverpool Dialect in Five Languages*. Liverpool: Scouse Press.

'Spion Kop'. 1906. *Liverpool Echo*. June 14th: 3.

Strong, H.A. 1896. 'Liverpool'. *Notes and Queries*. 8th series. Vol. IX: 233.

Tirebuck, William. 1891. *Dorrie: A Novel*. London: Longmans, Green and Co.

Tolkien, J.R.R. and E.V. Gordon. 1967. *Sir Gawain and the Green Knight*. Oxford: Clarendon.

Troughton, Thomas. 1810. *History of Liverpool. From the Earliest Authenticated Period Down to the Present Time*. Liverpool: Robinson.

Unwin, Frank. 1984. *Reflections on the Mersey Memoirs of the Twenties and Thirties*. Leighton Banastre: Gallery Press.

Urquhart, Thomas. 1653. *The first book of the works of Mr. Francis Rabelais, Doctor in Physick, containing five books of the lives, heroick deeds, and sayings of Gargantua, and his sonne Pantagruel*. London: Ratcliffe and Mottershead.

Vaux, James Hardy. 1819. *Memoirs of James Hardy Vaux*. London: Clowes.

Verstegan, Richard. 1605. *Restitution of Decayed Intelligence in Antiquities concerning the most noble and renowned English Nation*. Antwerp: Bruney.

Ward, Ned. 1707. *The Wooden World Dissected*. London: Moore.

Watson, Kevin. 2007. 'Is Scouse Getting Scouser? Phonological Change in Contemporary Liverpool English'. In Anthony Grant and Clive Grey. *The Mersey Sound: Liverpool's Language, People and Places*. Ormskirk: Open House Press: 215–41.

Webster, Noah. 1789. *Dissertations on the English Language*. Boston: Thomas.

Whatton, W.R. 1817. 'On the Etymology of the Word *Liverpool*'. *The Gentleman's Magazine*. Vol. LXXXVII, ii: 505–8.

Whittington-Egan, Richard. 1955a. 'Liverpool Dialect is Dying Out'. *Liverpool Echo*. April 14th: 6.

Whittington-Egan, Richard. 1955b. 'Is Liverpool Dialect Dying Out?'. In *Liverpool Colonnade*. Liverpool: Philip, Son and Nephew.

Witherspoon, John. 1781. (No title). *Pennsylvania Journal*. May 9th: 1.

Wittgenstein, Ludwig. 1967. *Philosophical Investigations*. Trans. G.E.M. Anscombe. Oxford: Blackwell.

Woollaston, Victoria. 2013. 'Scousers Have the "Least Intelligent and Least Trustworthy" Accent'. *Daily Mail Online*. https://www.dailymail. co.uk/sciencetech/article-2433201/Scousers-intelligent-trustworthy-accent--Devonians-friendliest.html. Downloaded November 8th, 2022.

Wyld, H.C. 1907. *The Growth of English*. London: Murray.

Wyld, H.C. and T. Oakes Hirst. 1911. *The Place Names of Lancashire: Their Origin and History*. London: Constable and Co.

INDEX OF NAMES

.